Where?
Ayeh?

REBBE NACHMAN

Published by
Breslov Research Institute
Jerusalem/New York

Copyright © 2023 BRESLOV RESEARCH INSTITUTE
ISBN 978-1-928822-09-7

Fourth edition

No part of this book may be translated, reproduced, stored in any retrieval system or transmitted, in any form or by any means, electronic, mechanical, photocopying, recording or otherwise, without prior permission in writing from the publisher.

For further information:
Breslov Research Institute
POB 5370, Jerusalem, Israel 91053
or:
Breslov Research Institute
POB 587, Monsey, NY 10952-0587

www.breslov.org
e-mail: info@breslov.org

Printed in Israel

"איה מקום כבודו"
(תיקוני זוהר י׳ כ"ה.)
"Where is the place of His glory"

In memory of
my Beloved Father

Solomon Garazi Lilo Z"L

Pillar of the Cuban Jewish
Sepharadic community and beyond.

Who always found joy
in everything.

May his Soul have an *aliyah*.

Your loving daughter,

Blanca Garazi Schoonover
Bracha *bat* **Esther**

Editor's Preface

Suppose you've tried hard—or even if you *haven't* tried—and when you take a long, truthful look at yourself, you feel as if you are further than ever from your goal. Should you fall into despair and give up?

"*Gevalt!*" cried Rebbe Nachman. "Don't give up! There is no despair!" The comfort and encouragement he gave are far from empty words. They are firmly grounded in the deepest foundations of Torah, as we see in his fundamental lesson of *Ayeh?*—"*Where* is the place of His glory?" (*Likutey Moharan* II, 12). One of the main themes of this lesson is that the places that seem furthest from God actually contain the most exalted life force of all.

This book presents a translation of the lesson of *Ayeh?* accompanied by selections from related teachings of Rebbe Nachman. These are followed by several extensive excerpts from *Likutey Halakhot* by Rebbe Nachman's closest pupil, Reb Noson. Reb Noson explores the many implications of *Ayeh?* over all areas of life, as well as the light it sheds on many teachings in the Torah and Rabbinic literature. Rebbe Nachman requested that we "turn the lessons into prayer" (*Likutey Moharan* II, 25). Accordingly, the book concludes with Reb Noson's prayer on *Ayeh?* in *Likutey Tefilot* II, 12.

In essence, *Ayeh?* teaches us how to draw light out of the darkest situations. As such, it is one of the main paths to genuine happiness and the sequel to *Azamra!* (Breslov Research Institute, 2012), which teaches how to attain happiness through "finding the good points." The final excerpt from *Likutey Halakhot* explores the interrelationship between the two lessons. For, "Two are better than one…for if they fall, the one will lift up his fellow" (Ecclesiastes 4:9-10).

The ideas in this book are very profound; some may seem obscure and remote on first acquaintance. It may take time to assimilate them and see how very close they actually are to our everyday lives. The best way to come to understand is through following the very simple idea behind the book *in practice*—by searching for God in all situations. With patience and persistence, you will certainly succeed.

May we merit to follow the two holy paths of *Ayeh?* and *Azamra!* at all times, and with their help, advance from level to level and from strength to strength, arousing God's love and compassion until He sends us our righteous Mashiach, speedily in our days. Amen.

And from there you will search for the Lord your God, and you will find Him, if you search after Him with all your heart and all your soul.

(Deuteronomy 4:29)

~

A crown is given to You, O Lord our God, by the throngs of angels above together with Your People, Israel, gathered below. They all praise You together with the threefold praise of holiness as revealed by the hand of Your prophet: "And they called one to the other and said, 'Holy, holy, holy is the Lord of Hosts, the whole earth is filled with His glory'" (Isaiah 6:3). His glory fills the universe, His ministering angels ask one another, *"Ayeh mekom kevodo?* **WHERE IS THE PLACE OF HIS GLORY?"** Those over against them praise Him and say, "Blessed is the glory of the Lord from His place" (Ezekiel 3:12).

(From the *Shabbat Musaf Kedushah*)

~

Every person must constantly advance from level to level. When the time comes for someone to advance from one level to the next, he must first experience a fall before he can rise up. The whole purpose of the fall is to prepare for the advance. So no matter how far you may fall, you should never allow yourself to be discouraged. Remain firm and resolute. In the end, the fall will be transformed into a great advance. This is its whole purpose. People think this only applies to those on very high levels who are continually advancing from level to level. But you should know that it holds true even for people on the lowest of levels. For God is good to all.

(*Likutey Moharan* I, 22)

An outstanding classic of Jewish religious literature, Likutey Moharan is a collection of Rebbe Nachman's major Torah lessons and the primary source book for all his principal teachings. These lessons were given on different occasions in Rebbe Nachman's life and were written down by his pupil, Reb Noson, under the Rebbe's direct supervision. With references ranging over the entire length and breadth of the Scriptures, Talmud, Midrash, Halakhah and Kabbalah, Likutey Moharan is especially noted for its brilliant exploration of the interrelationships between words and concepts in the Hebrew language.

The teaching of Ayeh? appears in Likutey Moharan II, 12. This lesson was given in the summer of 5568 (1808). The previous year, Rebbe Nachman left his hometown of Breslov for his dramatic and mysterious journey to Lemberg (see Azamra! for the significance of this journey). *He returned to Breslov in the summer of 5568, sick with tuberculosis, and often traveled to the outskirts of the city to take walks in the meadows with some of his followers. It was on one of these excursions that he revealed the lesson of Ayeh?* (Rebbe Nachman's Wisdom #144).

Ayeh?
Likutey Moharan II, 12

When a person follows his own ideas, he can fall into many errors and pitfalls and come to great evil. There are cases of people who have caused tremendous damage, like the famous great villains who led the entire world astray, all through their intelligence and cunning.

The essence of Judaism is to go in pure innocence and simplicity with no sophistication whatsoever. Make sure that whatever you do, God is there. Do not pay any regard to your own esteem. If something will enhance God's glory, do it. If not, then don't. This way, you can be certain you will never stumble.

Even if you fall into doubts, God forbid—and there are people who sink very low indeed and fall into all kinds of doubts and even have questions about God Himself—even so, the whole purpose of their downfall is so they should later rise up. The descent is for the sake of the ascent.

• God's Glory

For know that the root of the entire Creation is *glory*. Whatever God has created, He has done only for His glory. "Everything that is called by My Name and that I have created *for My glory*" (Isaiah 43:7; see

Yoma 38a). Since everything has been created for God's glory, it follows that His glory is the root of the entire Creation. And although everything is a unity, there are nevertheless gradations within the Creation. Each individual portion of the Creation contains its own unique glory, which is the root of that portion. This idea is contained in the teaching of the Rabbis: "With Ten Utterances the world was created. But couldn't it have been created with only one? The reason it was created with Ten Utterances was for the purpose of reward and punishment" (*Avot* 5:1). Each Utterance has its own unique glory, which is its root—for glory is the root of everything, as we have seen. "In His Temple everything declares, 'Glory!'" (Psalms 29:9)—each utterance is a garment expressing God's glory, the glory with which the world was created. For, "the whole earth is filled with His glory" (Isaiah 6:3).

What about sin and evil? God's glory is *not* present there, for, "I will not give My glory to another" (ibid., 42:8). There is a limit to the glory, preventing it from spreading there. Even though "the whole earth is filled with His glory," there is nevertheless a limit when it reaches those places, so that it will not extend to them—for, "I will not give My glory to another." There is a limit to each portion of the glory clothed in all the Ten Utterances through which the world was created.

This limit prevents the glory from spreading to the areas beyond the bounds of holiness, the "outside places."

But know that in spite of this, they, too, undoubtedly receive their vitality from God. Even the "filthy places," even idolatrous temples, necessarily derive their life force from God. But know that they receive it from the Hidden Utterance of *Bereshit*, "In the beginning" (Genesis 1:1; see *Chidushei Aggadot* on *Shabbat* 104a). This Utterance includes all the others and all of them derive their vitality from it. The glory of the Hidden Utterance is concealed and hidden to the ultimate degree. It is from there that they derive their life force. It is impossible for the "filthy places" to receive their vitality from the revealed Utterances for the reason that, "I will not give My glory to another." Only from the Hidden Utterance, which is concealed to the ultimate degree, do they receive vitality. This is something that is impossible to understand with human reason, and we may not delve into it.

• The Search

When a person sinks to these "filthy places," God forbid, he is filled with doubts, questions and confusion. But then, when he starts examining himself and sees how far he is from God's glory, and begins asking and searching *Ayeh?*—"*Where* is the place of His glory?"—this is itself the solution. He sees for himself that he is far from God's glory, having sunk to such places. When he asks *Ayeh?*—"*Where?*"—this is his way to rise up and transform the descent into a great ascent. Because the purpose of the descent is for the sake of the ascent.

Ayeh?—"*Where* is the place of His glory?" This alludes to the exalted glory of the highest Utterance, the Hidden Utterance of *Bereshit*, which is the source of the life force of these places. And so, when a person searches in earnest, *Ayeh?*—"*Where* is the place of His glory?"—through this itself he comes back and rises to the highest glory, *Ayeh?*—which because of its great concealment gives life to these places. Now that he has fallen there and then searches *Ayeh?*—"*Where* is the place of His glory?"—through this he comes back and connects himself to there. He injects his very downfall itself with vitality and is able to rise (Hebrew: *oleh*) to the most exalted heights.

This is the concept of the *olah*-sacrifice, the burnt-offering (all of which ascended to God since the whole animal was burned on the altar). The *OLaH*-sacrifice comes to atone for the doubts in a person's heart. It is written, "And that which comes up (Hebrew: *ha-OLeH*) into your mind" (Ezekiel 20:32)—namely, thoughts. From this verse the Rabbis learned that the *olah*-sacrifice atones for the doubts in one's heart (see *Vayikra Rabbah* 7:3).

"My heart pounds" (Psalms 38:11)—for there is a *kelipah*, a husk, that surrounds and contorts the heart with all kinds of crookedness and confusion. This is the kelipah of *nogah* (which contains good and evil, revelation and concealment). The Hebrew word for "pounds," *s'charchar*, derives from the Aramaic for "roundabout." Similarly, the "brightness (*nogah*) was roundabout" (Ezekiel 1:4). The reason for the Aramaic form in the verse in Psalms is that the kelipah of nogah is bound up with the concept of *targum*, translation—specifically, the Aramaic translation of the Torah. (See *Likutey Moharan* I, 19. A translation conveys part but not all of the original, concealing as well as revealing. A translation may be very misleading.) When a person falls into such doubts—the "filthy places"—and then searches and cries out *Ayeh?*—"*Where* is the place of His glory?"—this in itself is his remedy, for through it he returns to the supreme glory which is expressed in *Ayeh?*

Ayeh? expresses the idea of the *olah*-sacrifice, as it is written, "But where (*ayeh*) is the lamb for the *olah*-sacrifice?" (Genesis 22:7). Asking *Ayeh?*—"*Where?*"—is in itself the "lamb for the *olah*-sacrifice," as it resolves and atones for all the doubts in a person's heart stemming from the "filthy places." For it is through asking *Ayeh?*—"*Where?*"—that he is healed and rises out of them.

Thus the *Tikkuney Zohar* teaches that the Hebrew word *BeReShiYT* contains the letters *BaRa TaYiSh*, "He created a kid" (*Tikkun Tinyana* 4:1), alluding to the "lamb for the *olah*-sacrifice," which is made through asking *Ayeh?*, embodying as it does *Bereshit*, the Hidden Utterance.

• *Teshuvah:* Asking is the Answer

This is the concept of *teshuvah*, repentance and returning to God. The essence of *teshuvah* is when a person earnestly searches for God's glory. He sees in himself that he is far from God's glory. He yearns for it. He asks. He labors and toils. *Ayeh?*—"*Where* is the place of His glory?" This in itself is his answer, his repentance and his remedy. Understand this well.

There is much more to this. For when a person goes on a journey, or travels along spiritual paths, the Torah goes before him. "When you walk it will lead you" (Proverbs 6:22; also *Avot* 6:10). Many different concepts are involved in this, depending on the individual and his level in Torah. Before each revelation of Torah arise the doubts we have spoken of. For example, before a person can develop original Torah ideas, he must experience all kinds of doubts and confusions before he achieves the necessary clarity. These doubts correspond to the Tree of the Knowledge of Good and Evil, which embodies the concept of nogah. But when he reaches the Torah itself, this is the Tree of Life.

• Rising Up

"If someone asks you, 'Where is your God?' tell him, 'In the big city of Rome'" (*Yerushalmi, Ta'anit* 1:1). Even in places filled with idols and cults, God is hidden there. If you sink to such places, God forbid, as soon as you begin to search *Ayeh?*—"*Where* is the place of His glory?"—with this you give yourself life from the life force of holiness. The vitality of the *kelipot*, the forces of evil, derives only from the concealment, from the fact that God is so totally hidden that there is no awareness of Him at all. But as soon as you begin to search, "*Where* is the place of His glory?" it indicates that you at least know that God exists, only He is hidden and concealed, and this is why you are searching *Ayeh?*—"*Where* is the place of His glory?"

This is how you can give yourself new life in the place you have sunken to. *Ayeh?* refers to the Hidden Utterance from which all things derive their vitality. The vitality of the kelipot derives from the concealment itself. Because now you vitalize yourself with the life force of holiness in the very place you have sunken to—by earnestly searching *Ayeh?*—"*Where* is the place of His glory?"—afterwards you can lift yourself out of there completely and reach holiness in a place where God's glory is revealed. For the essence of holiness is that God's glory should be revealed. Blessed be God forever. Amen. Amen.

Related Teachings

Many of the ideas in *Ayeh?* are connected with ideas found elsewhere in Rebbe Nachman's teachings. Here is a selection of excerpts shedding light on some of the main concepts in *Ayeh?*:

• Simplicity

People should throw aside all their sophisticated ideas and serve God with purity and simplicity. Action is the main thing, not study. You should see to it that your practical achievements are greater than your intellectual development. When it comes to serving God, even someone whose head is filled with genuine wisdom should put it all aside and serve God with purity and simplicity. At times it may even be necessary to behave in a way that seems mad in order to serve God. We may have to roll about in all kinds of mud and mire to serve God and fulfill His commandments. When one's love of God is strong enough, he becomes a "precious and beloved son," and God will show him abundant love and compassion, permitting him to investigate the hidden treasuries of the King until he will learn the deepest secrets of all—why the righteous suffer and the wicked prosper, and so on. He will then be worthy of the secrets of Torah.

(*Likutey Moharan* II, 5:15)

● Revelation

The main thing is to nullify every one of your personality traits. You must strive to do so until you have totally obliterated your ego, rendering it into absolute nothingness before God. Begin with one trait and annihilate it completely. Then work on your other traits, one at a time, until they are totally nonexistent. As you nullify your own personality, God's glory will begin to shine through and be revealed.

It is written, "And the earth was alight with His glory" (Ezekiel 43:2). God's glory is like light. The larger an object, the greater its shadow. A thin rod casts a very small shadow, while a more substantial object casts a larger shadow. A great building will cast a still larger shadow. As more light is obstructed, a greater shadow is cast. The same is true of God's glory. The material obstructs the spiritual and casts a shadow. The denser an object, the deeper a shadow it will cast.

When you are bound to an emotion or desire, it obstructs God's glory and casts a shadow. God's light is then hidden from you. But as you nullify these emotions and desires, you also remove this shadow. And as the shadow departs, the light of God's glory is revealed. When a man is worthy of annihilating the shadow completely and making it into absolute nothingness, then God's glory is revealed to all the earth. There is no obstructing shadow, and the light can shine through in all its glory.

(*Rebbe Nachman's Wisdom* #136)

• Falling

Each time a person emerges from one level in order to rise up to the next, the kelipot attack him again in the form of temptations, fantasies, strange thoughts, confusions and all kinds of other obstacles. They range themselves against him and refuse to allow him to enter the gates of holiness. Many sincere people get very discouraged when they suddenly find themselves confronted by all these temptations and obstacles. They start thinking they must have fallen from their previous level because for some time now they had not experienced all these temptations to the same degree. [The temptations lay] dormant. But they should understand that what they are experiencing is not a fall. The time has come for them to advance from one level to the next. This is the reason why these temptations and obstacles rear their heads again. Whenever this happens, it takes a lot of strength and courage not to lose hope and to master all the temptations and obstacles anew.

(*Likutey Moharan* I, 25)

When a person falls from his level, he should know that this is something sent to him from Heaven. The whole purpose of the apparent rejection is to draw him closer. The fall is meant to spur him to make new efforts to come closer to God. The thing to do is to make an entirely new start. Start serving God as if you had never started in your whole life. This is one of the most basic principles of serving God. We must literally begin all over again, every day.

(Likutey Moharan I, 261)

• Doubts

There are many searching questions about God. It is only fitting and proper that this should be so. Indeed, such questions enhance the greatness of God and show His exaltedness. God is so great and exalted that He is beyond our ability to understand Him. It is obviously impossible for us to understand His ways with our limited human intelligence. Inevitably there will be things that baffle us, and it is only fitting that that should be so. If God's ways were in accordance with the demands of our meager understanding, there would be no difference between His understanding and ours, God forbid.

(Likutey Moharan II, 52)

Falling in Order to Rise

The major theme of *Ayeh?* is what to do when we fall. Many times, we feel low and far from God. Then we have to *search* for God. Reb Noson takes up this theme in the following extract from *Likutey Halakhot*, his eight-volume work discussing the laws of the *Shulchan Arukh* in light of Rebbe Nachman's teachings. This excerpt is from *Choshen Mishpat, Hilkhot Gevi'at Chov Mihayetomim* 3. Rebbe Nachman taught that the fall comes for the very purpose of helping us to rise up (see above, p. 21). Indeed, spiritual progress is impossible without falling. Reb Noson explains why this is so: The fall forces us to search *Ayeh?*—"*Where* is the place of His glory?" And the level of *Ayeh?*—the very source of the Creation—is the source of the new energies we need in order to rise up.

The material demands on our lives necessarily produce times when we are far from God's glory. Reb Noson shows us how to overcome the distance by giving the Torah, the revealed glory of God, pride of place in our lives. The Torah provides us with a firm base on which to fight the challenges of life and find God wherever we are.

Reb Noson then widens the discussion from the path of the individual to the journey of the Jewish People from exile to redemption. In the light of *Ayeh?* we see that exile is far from a purposeless episode. Rather, it is the necessary preparation for an ascent to the highest level of spirituality. This is what we await now, as we prepare for the coming of Mashiach.

Reb Noson writes:

The teaching of *Ayeh?* is relevant to people on all different levels, especially those who have become detached from religion. If you have fallen down badly, there is really no other way to give yourself new life. You must search for God where you are, in your actual situation, there in the place you have fallen to. This is how you can climb out of your low and rise way above.

However, *Ayeh?* also applies to those who have already attained a high degree of spirituality. All people need to follow this teaching, because everyone must constantly move forward from level to level; it is no good to stand still. When the time comes to progress from one level to the next, you must necessarily experience a fall before you can rise up. The moment you actually fall, you are far from God. His glory becomes concealed from you. This is when you have to search *Ayeh?*—"*Where* is the place of His glory?" Only by searching can you rise and attain the higher level.

It is only possible to move from level to level through *Ayeh?*, which is the highest Utterance, the Hidden

Utterance of *Bereshit*, from which all Ten Utterances derive. The reason is that when you move from one level to the next, in effect you become a new person with new spiritual powers. All your energies are renewed when you leave your previous level and enter the next. The only way to renew yourself and go forward is by first going back. You have to go back to the ultimate root—which is *Ayeh?*, the root of all Ten Utterances through which the world was created. As such, *Ayeh?* contains all the worlds, all the souls, and all the levels in the world. This explains why there has to be a fall before you can move forward. Before you can rise, you must first go back and attach yourself to the ultimate root of *Ayeh?*, which contains all the levels in the world. Only here is it possible to receive the new spiritual energies needed to rise to your new level. There has to be a fall because it is through falling that you are spurred into searching *Ayeh?* When you search properly, you can rise to the ultimate heights of *Ayeh?*, the root of all, and then you can draw from there the new life and energy you need to achieve the higher level.

• Torah and a Worldly Occupation

It is good to combine Torah study with a worldly occupation, because the effort they both involve makes sin be forgotten *(Avot 2:2)*.

The spiritual work of a Jew is divided into two categories, with the emphasis sometimes on one and sometimes on the other. The first category is studying Torah and keeping the mitzvot. This aspect of our spiritual work centers around the revealed glory of God, the glory that fills the world—for "the whole world is filled with His glory." God's revealed glory refers to the Ten Utterances through which the world was created and in which God's glory is clothed. These Utterances are revealed in the Torah and mitzvot as a whole and are encompassed in the Ten Commandments, which correspond to the Ten Utterances. The whole purpose of keeping the holy Torah is to reveal God's glory, which is the root of the Torah, as the Rabbis indicated when they said, "Glory is none other than Torah" (*Avot* 6:3). We must occupy ourselves with Torah and mitzvot constantly so as to reveal God's glory, until the entire world is filled with His glory. This is the idea of the passage at the beginning of the lesson of *Ayeh?* which speaks about how everyone must always examine what they are intending to do to see if it will enhance God's glory. If it does, they should do it; if not, then not. All our actions should enhance God's glory.

But it is impossible to be attached to the Torah every moment of the day and night without interruption. Sometimes it is necessary to take a break for a while, as the Talmud teaches, "There are times when the best way to keep the Torah is by leaving off Torah" (*Menachot* 99a). Besides, people have their work obligations and other material needs. When they are thus occupied they do not see God's glory, because God's glory is mainly revealed in the Torah and mitzvot. During the times you are removed from the Torah, you have to inspire yourself with the second kind of spiritual work: searching for God's hidden glory through *Ayeh?*— "*Where* is the place of His glory?" Then you will be able to draw inspiration wherever you are, regardless of the situation. Even if you get into bad ways and find yourself in the worst possible situation, you must still take yourself in hand and follow the teaching of *Ayeh?*, searching for God in every way you can. Through this you will be able to rise way above to the level of *Ayeh?* itself. This level atones for all sins, and by searching *Ayeh?* you can make amends for everything, as taught in the lesson.

"It is good to combine Torah study with a worldly occupation, because the effort they both involve makes sin be forgotten" (*Avot* 2:2). "Torah" and "a worldly occupation" refer to the two kinds of spiritual work. The first involves the *revealed* glory of God that fills all the world and manifests in the Torah and mitzvot. The second applies to worldly affairs—business and other mundane matters, which are not intrinsically holy and where God's glory is not directly visible. Yet we are still obliged to attend to them, and then we have to search for God's glory and find life and inspiration through *Ayeh?*, the Hidden Utterance, which is the source of all things. *Ayeh?* is so concealed that even sin and the forces of evil draw their life force from there. By searching, "*Where* is the place of His glory?" it is possible to rise to the great heights of *Ayeh?*, the very roots of holiness. Here all sin and all the forces of evil are nullified. This is indicated in the Mishnah when it says, "the effort they both involve makes sin be forgotten." The two kinds of spiritual work, Torah and worldly affairs, are both necessary, and together they nullify sin and the forces of evil.

Pursuing worldly occupations by and for themselves is valueless. Granted, it is possible to search for God there, too, and come to the heights of *Ayeh?* But worldly affairs involve considerable risks. It is all too easy to get trapped by them and go astray. This is because worldly affairs and business pursuits derive their life from *Ayeh?* Firstly, the holiness of *Ayeh?* is greatly concealed, and secondly, precisely because of its concealment, *Ayeh?* is also the source of the power of all the forces of unholiness, making their influence very potent in the world of mundane affairs. For both these reasons, it is very easy to get so caught up in business and other material pursuits that you come to forget God completely. "Your silver and gold will multiply...and your heart will be lifted up and you will forget the Lord your God" (Deuteronomy 8:13-14). Because holiness lies in a state of concealment in worldly affairs, the one who is involved in mundane pursuits must search for God very intensely. Only through searching is it possible to find Him and rise to the level of *Ayeh?* Failure to do so properly may bring one to forget God completely.

Therefore, someone who is involved in business and other material affairs should be sure to set fixed times for Torah study. The Torah should be his first priority, while worldly affairs should take second place. God's glory is revealed in the holy Torah. If you immerse yourself in the Torah, then even when you go out into the world to attend to your material needs and business pursuits, you will not get trapped. You will still be able to search for God's glory, because by giving the Torah priority in your life you will have made it your constant endeavor to reveal God's glory at all times. Even when you are far from God's glory while engaged in worldly affairs, you will still search *Ayeh?*—"*Where* is the place of His glory?" This way, you will be able to rise to the ultimate heights.

It is equally impossible to be occupied only in Torah to the exclusion of all worldly involvement. You must always be moving from level to level, and in order to do so, you have to fall first before you can rise higher. In your lows, the only way to revive yourself is by searching for God's glory. This is the spiritual work of the second kind—involvement with worldly affairs, such as making a living. This is when you have to *search* for God's glory in order to rise to the ultimate heights of *Ayeh?* through which all sins are nullified. This explains how "the effort they both involve makes sin be forgotten." Through the combination of these two types of spiritual work, sin and evil are nullified.

• Traveling

Rebbe Nachman alludes to the basic concept of this Mishnah at the end of the lesson of *Ayeh?* where he speaks about traveling. When a person goes on a journey, the Torah goes before him, and before each revelation of Torah there are doubts and confusions. The two categories in the Mishnah are Torah and worldly occupations, which correspond to "when you sit in your house" and "when you go on the way" (Deuteronomy 6:7). The practice of laboring in Torah study is compared to "sitting in your house" because the holiness of Torah is permanent, like a house; it is fixed and established forever. One who immerses himself in Torah study tries to reveal God's glory, which is the foundation of the world. In contrast, one who is estranged from the Torah is separated from God's glory; he is called "a fugitive and a wanderer" (Genesis 4:14). This represents the idea of "going on the way." Such a person has no fixed place. He roams and wanders, and no one knows where his place is; today it is here, tomorrow somewhere else. Therefore, *"Where is the place of His glory?"* is connected to the idea of a worldly occupation in the Mishnah. The Hebrew expression for a worldly occupation is *derekh eretz*, the *way* of the world. So many business activities involve traveling. People turn into "fugitives and wanderers" in search of a livelihood. When we are involved in worldly affairs, we must *search* for God's glory. And so it is written, "He wanders around for bread—*'Where* is it?'" (Job 15:23).

This idea of traveling epitomizes the exile of the Jewish People. The exile turned the Jews into wanderers and fugitives in the Diaspora. "Like a bird wandering from her nest, so is a man who wanders from his place" (Proverbs 27:8). The wandering of the individual and the wandering of the Jewish People are one concept. In exile, we must search more than ever for God's glory, constantly asking *Ayeh?*—"*Where* is the place of His glory?" If we search for God, He will certainly help us find Him, as we are promised in the Torah: "God will scatter you among the nations…and from there you will search for the Lord your God and you will find Him, if you search after Him with all your heart and all your soul, in your distress when all these troubles befall you" (Deuteronomy 4:27-30).

This holds true especially in our time, as we approach the end of the exile and stand poised on the threshold of the Messianic age. Godliness is concealed more powerfully than ever beneath thousands upon thousands of layers. All the prophets from Moses onward, and even the Patriarchs themselves, foresaw and prophesied the dire troubles of the Jewish People at the end of days. Worst of all is the spiritual crisis—the tremendous gulf that separates us from God to a degree unparalleled in all of Jewish history. Not that we lack material difficulties. The material problems of our times are acute. Yet previous generations also endured endless material problems and suffering, including expulsions, migrations, persecutions and massacres. But when the prophets and sages contemplated the birth pangs of Mashiach with such foreboding, saying, "Let it come, but let me not see it" (*Sanhedrin* 98b), what chilled them was the depth of the *spiritual* crisis—the unbearable concealment of Godliness.

We find ourselves bereft of truly outstanding leaders like the great Tzaddikim of previous generations. Throughout the world, falsehood grows stronger and stronger while truth is fragmented. There is indeed a proliferation of truth—but only in the sense that the truth has been divided, with innumerable groups of people all claiming that the truth is on their side (cf. *Sanhedrin* 97a). Deep down, they are aware of their own inadequacies. Yet this does not stop them from boasting about how they have found new ways of getting close to God. Many have been led astray as a result, losing touch with the authentic Torah way that our ancestors always followed, free of sophistication and "new discoveries." Falsehood pushes itself forward in every possible way, "and they dash truth down to the ground" (Daniel 8:12).

Most serious of all is the rampant secularism coupled with a predominantly materialistic attitude towards life. This is the outlook dominating the education of the great majority of Jewish youth today. All the emphasis is on secular education, with the result that tender souls are trapped in a vicious network of ideas that alienates them from the spirituality which is the life source of the Jewish People. Spiritual death is far worse than physical death! If our hearts were sincerely turned to God like those of the saintly Jews of previous generations, we would be falling on our faces and beating our heads against the wall day and night at the thought of the catastrophe facing our youth. It is plain for all to see that the emphasis on secular studies at the expense of serious religious education has produced generations of scoffers who are alienated from the Torah and are totally removed from the traditions of Jewish sanctity and purity. It seems impossible to bring them back, for "all who go into her (i.e., secularism) will not return" (Proverbs 2:19).

The prophets long ago foresaw this terrible proliferation of spiritual troubles, as when Daniel wrote, "Many shall purify themselves and make themselves white and be refined, but the wicked will do wickedly and none of the wicked will understand; but those who are wise will understand" (Daniel 12:10). Blessed is he who can put his trust in God in times like these and take strength in Him. Nothing can equal the traditional path of truth and simplicity our fathers always traveled, raising their children with God's Torah, the Oral Torah (the Talmud and the Codes) and the Written Torah. But to put all the emphasis on the Written Torah to the total exclusion of the Oral Torah is a path fraught with danger. Those intellectuals who charted the direction for the education of so many Jewish children today claimed they wanted to give a new emphasis to Bible studies, and ended up eliminating religious studies from the curriculum altogether. They wanted their pupils to know about exotic places and unusual biological phenomena, but when it came to the details of Torah law, they were indifferent. May God take pity on us and our children, and on the remnant of the House of Israel, and save us from them.

At the climax of this final exile, therefore, it is essential for everyone to follow the teaching of *Ayeh?* at all times, constantly searching for God's glory in all places. If we search properly, we will undoubtedly find Him. This applies to everyone, regardless of how low he may be or what he may have gone through in his life. Even if you think you have made no progress at all, you should still try to get a grip on yourself and keep searching for God in the actual situation in which you find yourself. Even if you have descended to the worst possible places, the "filthy places" that are cut off from God's glory—for, "I will not give My glory to another" (Isaiah 42:8)—you should still make every effort to search *Ayeh?*—"*Where* is the place of His glory?" Eventually you will succeed, and you will rise to the ultimate heights of *Ayeh?*, the Hidden Utterance, which is the source of the vitality of all the Ten Utterances, all the worlds, all the souls and all the levels.

• In the Wilderness

After the Torah was given, the Children of Israel wandered about in the wilderness for forty years, and all the time the Sanctuary traveled with them. There God spoke with Moses, and from the mouth of Moses the Children of Israel learned Torah. The entire Torah is encompassed within the Ten Commandments, which embody the Ten Utterances through which God's glory is revealed. The entire Torah and all ten divisions of glory derive from the Hidden Utterance of *Bereshit—Ayeh?* This is the source of the Torah, the source of glory, and the source of the Ten Utterances.

Any revelation of Torah you attain, whether in your understanding of the Torah itself or your understanding of the meaning of your spiritual work (prayer, the mitzvot, etc.), is a "Giving of the Torah." All such revelations are necessarily preceded by a period of confusion. One finds himself tormented by doubts and plagued with obstacles and difficulties, physical desires, and all kinds of other distractions. They all derive from the remote places that draw their life force from the very concealment of the Hidden Utterance of *Ayeh?* When they attack, and it seems impossible to find a way out, you must ask and search *Ayeh?—"Where is the place of His glory?"* Then your fall into confusion serves its purpose, making it possible for you to rise to the level of *Ayeh?*, the Hidden Utterance, the very root of the Torah and all Ten Utterances. You can now draw Torah from this exalted source—for this is the root of the entire Torah.

The revelation of God's glory is a creation out of nothing—from *ayin*, nothing, to *yesh*, being. The source of the power that gives rise to all the glory, and the source of the Torah and all Ten Utterances, is *Ayeh?*, the Hidden Utterance, expressed in the word *Bereshit*. *Bereshit* is the first word of the Torah and the place from which all the rest of the Torah follows. It is from the very hiddenness and mystery of *Ayeh?* that the forces of evil and impurity receive their vitality. From here they derive their power to hide God's glory, sometimes even completely, and to put doubts, confusion and even atheism into man's heart. This is the source of the power of the evil inclination, which is called "an *other* god." Yet despite having become caught up in all this, you then ask *Ayeh?*—"*Where* is the place of His glory?"—you can then rise to the very root of holiness, the root of the Torah, the level of *Ayeh?*—*Bereshit*—and from there gain a new revelation of Torah.

Now we can understand why the Torah had to be given in the wilderness and not anywhere else, and only following the exile in Egypt. At the height of their slavery (spiritual and physical), the Children of Israel cried out to God (cf. Exodus 3:9). They had no idea at all what they should do to escape. Accordingly, they resorted to the traditional art of their fathers—crying out to God, searching and waiting to discover God's glory. This initiated their liberation. They went into the wilderness, "a place of snakes, serpents and scorpions, of thirst" (Deuteronomy 8:15)—a place that is removed from God's glory. There, of all places, they searched for God, until finally they received the Torah itself. Their decline achieved its purpose, culminating in their ascent. By searching in the "wilderness"—in the remote places—we attain Torah revelations, because the root of Torah is *Ayeh?*, which is to be found by searching.

• Doubts

Prior to the giving of the Torah, the Children of Israel fell into doubts. They asked, "Is (*yesh*) God among us, or not (*ayin*)?" (Exodus 17:7). The *Zohar* explains that they really wanted to know whether the holiness that dwelled among them was that designated as *yesh*, or the holiness called *ayin* (Zohar II, 64b). *Yesh* refers to God's revealed glory—for, "the whole earth is filled with His glory"—while *ayin* refers to the level of *Ayeh?* At the time, the Children of Israel had no water. Their suffering caused them to fall into doubts and they did not know if God was in their midst. This was the moment God brought Amalek against them (Exodus 17:8).

As long as the evil inclination lies more or less dormant, it is human nature to weaken in our search for God. Only when faced with an all-out attack are our spiritual powers aroused, bringing us to search in earnest, "*Where* is the place of His glory?" This explains why the war with Amalek occurred immediately before the Giving of the Torah. Amalek was the embodiment of the "filth of the serpent," epitomizing the "filthy places" where it is impossible to find God in any way. The only thing to do there is to cry out loudly to God and search, "Where *is* His glory?"

"Whenever Moses raised his hand, Israel prevailed" (Exodus 17:11). "As long as Moses raised his hand and Israel looked up to Heaven, they were victorious" (*Rosh HaShanah* 29a). Why did Moses raise his hand instead of telling the Israelites explicitly to turn their hearts to God? The answer is that at the height of such an attack by the "serpent" and the "filthy places," it is impossible even to speak of God's glory, because it cannot be found there. The only thing left is to hint, as Moses did with his hands, raising them upwards as a sign that the Israelites should lift their hearts upwards and search *Ayeh?* This was the key to the Israelite victory. They rose to the ultimate level of *Ayeh?* and therefore received the Torah immediately afterwards, because the roots of the Torah are in *Ayeh?*

When Moses first went to Pharaoh to ask him to free the Children of Israel, Pharaoh answered by imposing more burdens upon the people. He increased the oppression so much that even Moses was led to question God: "Why have You treated this people badly?" (Exodus

5:22). The oppression intensified because the liberation had to stem from the level of *Ayeh?*, which is the "final Jubilee," the fiftieth gate, the source of the true freedom of the Jewish People. Therefore, at the climax of the exile, on the very threshold of the liberation, God hid Himself so completely that even Moses himself was unable to understand His ways. That was why Moses asked this question. He was asking *Ayeh?*—"*Where* is the place of His glory?" Where is God's promise to redeem them? Now they are suffering more than ever! And this was precisely how the liberation came about. Through Moses' searching, God revealed Himself to him more fully than ever (Exodus 6:2-8), and in the end, God redeemed the Children of Israel through Moses.

Thus the end of the lesson of *Ayeh?* indicates that even the greatest Tzaddikim must face doubts before they can attain new revelations of Torah. These doubts lead them to ask *Ayeh?*, and this is what brings about the revelation. The liberation from Egypt was itself a "revelation of Torah," since it marked the beginning of the process that culminated in the Giving of the Torah on Sinai. Moreover, at the time of the Exodus itself, the Children of Israel received several mitzvot, because the most important facet of redemption is the freeing of the soul so it can come close to God. This is the "Giving of the Torah."

• Never Give Up!

Every exile of the Jewish People was followed by a revelation of Torah. After the redemption from Egypt came the revelation at Sinai. After the Babylonian exile came the revelation in the time of Mordekhai and Esther. And so it will be after the present exile. We will then receive the greatest revelation of all, because the main revelation of the Torah is destined to occur at the coming of the Mashiach. Through our very exile among the nations—in the "filthy places"—we are brought to search *Ayeh?* "And *from there* you will search for the Lord your God" (Deuteronomy 4:29). The search itself will bring us to the greatest ascent of all—to the level of *Ayeh?*, the root of the Torah itself.

Today, at the end of this final exile, the concealment has become deeper than ever. God is hidden from us in the "concealment within the concealment" (see *Likutey Moharan* I, 56:3). Our only hope is to do everything in our power to search *Ayeh?*—"*Where* is the place of His glory?"—sighing with longing for spiritual freedom. The intensity of the exile serves this purpose alone: to bring us to search. Because now we have to rise to the highest level of all to achieve the final redemption. That is why this exile has been so long and painful, to the point that everybody is wondering what happened to God's promise and when the long-awaited end will come. By searching, we will come to *Ayeh?*, and then we will attain the final redemption.

It is impossible to communicate in writing how firm and persistent you must be. Don't let yourself be discouraged. Even if you feel you have fallen to the lowest hell, don't give up. You are still capable of doing something good. Just don't get discouraged, or you won't even do what you still can! The Rebbe emphasized this time and time again. Some of his most wonderful teachings center on this idea. But the point must be repeated again and again, because people get so discouraged they imagine it doesn't apply to them. Each one thinks his own situation is so impossible, his physical desires so strong and the obstacles so great that he can never come close to God. The Rebbe vehemently disagreed. "*Gevalt!* Don't despair!" he cried, drawing out the word *Gevalt* (*Likutey Moharan* II, 78).

Everyone can succeed and come close to God through this lesson alone. Search and search in every way you can. Eventually you must succeed, and then you will see that no effort is ever lost. Even the slightest gesture of an effort is most precious in God's eyes. Each little motion is a part of the remedy…until in the end, you will rise to the greatest heights.

Making a Living

In the previous section, Reb Noson discussed the challenges of making a living and how to meet them. In the following excerpt (*Likutey Halakhot, Orach Chaim, Hilkhot Eruvey Techumin* 6:24, 27), he addresses the same subject from a different angle, examining the source from which our livelihood comes. We may be able to trace the immediate chain of events that brings us our income—be it salary, profit, a sudden windfall or whatever. We must be aware, however, that everything in the world is governed by God down to the smallest detail. Beyond the immediate causes rests a higher source from which our livelihood derives. Knowing this, we are better able to develop our trust that whatever we need will be sent to us when the time is right, regardless of whether or not we can see it on the horizon.

Reb Noson writes:

A person's income is symbolized by the idea of manna. At its root, the manna derives from the Hidden Utterance of *Ayeh?*, "for they did not know what it was" (Exodus 16:15). Similarly, the Rabbis taught, "A person's livelihood depends not on his merit but on mazel." Mazel alludes to Keter, the Crown, the highest of the Sefirot, which is itself the Hidden Utterance.

Owing to its exalted source, the manna involved many trials for the Jewish People. They complained before it came down (ibid., 16:2), and afterwards they were tested by being told not to leave any over until the morning (ibid., 16:19). God said He was sending the manna "in order that I may try them to see if they will go by My Torah" (ibid., 16:4), and Moses said, "He afflicted you to test you…He afflicted you to let you hunger, and He fed you the manna, which neither you nor your fathers knew" (Deuteronomy 8:2-3). The Hidden Utterance from which the manna derived is the source of man's trials in life, because the forces of evil draw their strength from it. Man has to pass through these "places" to be tested. If he succeeds in searching for God even there, he can rise to supreme heights.

Precisely because the manna—namely, one's livelihood—derives from this exalted source, earning a living is one of the main tests a person endures in life. Before he can receive his living from the Hidden Utterance, he must pass through the "filthy places" where it is impossible to see Godliness and where all kinds of difficulties and confusions arise. But if he stands up to the test and succeeds in searching for God even there, his fall becomes transformed into a great ascent and he draws his livelihood from the Hidden Utterance.

We can understand why some of the Children of Israel stumbled and complained against God before the manna came down. They were overwhelmed by the doubts and confusions they first encountered, all of which arose from the heavy concealment of the Hidden Utterance. The majority, however, acted correctly, asking and searching for God's glory until the manna came down.

There is a deep meaning to the tests that came afterwards—"in order that I may try them"—to see if the Children of Israel would fulfill the related mitzvot which included not leaving any of the manna over until the next morning. Precisely because a person's livelihood—his manna—comes from such an exalted and concealed source, as soon as it enters this material world the light from which it derives immediately becomes hidden again. This light cannot be apprehended through reason, only through faith. So as soon as the manna came down for one day, it was hard for the Children of Israel to believe that it would come down the next day as well. The forces hiding Godliness also derive their life force from the Hidden Utterance, and constantly assail the heart anew. This explains why some of the Children of Israel did not stand up to the test. They found it hard to believe that the manna would come down again the next day, so they kept some of it overnight. "And it bred worms and rotted" (Exodus 16:20)—because the forces of evil gained control. In truth, the manna for each day could only come down that day. Each of the six days of Creation has its own Utterance through which God brought about the creation of that day. Between each day lies a boundary, a "contraction," whose source lies in the concealment of the Hidden Utterance. This is the darkness preceding each day, as in, "It was evening and it was morning of the first/second/third day" (Genesis 1).

In the darkness of night, "all the beasts of the forest creep forth" (Psalms 104:20). The forces of evil gain control at night since their power derives from darkness—the concealment of the Hidden Utterance. Each day, only enough manna came down for that day to inspire the Children of Israel to lift their eyes upwards. It is impossible to draw blessing from the Hidden Utterance for all the days at once, because this would violate the limits placed between each individual day, giving too much power to the forces of evil. "Lifting the eyes upwards" refers to searching *Ayeh?*—"*Where* is the place of His glory?" Each day, one must search again so as to bring down the livelihood for the next day.

"Moses said to Aaron, 'Take a jar and put an *omer* of manna in it, and lay it before God to be kept throughout your generations'" (Exodus 16:33). A portion of the manna was to be kept as a memorial because today, too, our livelihood comes to us in the same way as the manna. This is something everyone should realize. It is true there are differences. The manna came down as ready food, day by day, while today each individual receives his livelihood in a manner uniquely suited to him. Some people make enough profit on one deal to support themselves for a whole year; others receive their income each month or each week; and still others barely receive what they need day by day. There are innumerable distinctions, yet even so, everyone receives his livelihood like the manna in the sense that it derives from the Hidden Utterance. We therefore have to pass through the remote places and undergo all the trials of making a living honestly, without deceit or theft and without succumbing to the craving for wealth. All these tests derive from the forces of evil. Then, as soon as anyone receives his livelihood or comes into some extra money, the light is immediately concealed from him and he does not know where his income will come from in the future. Sometimes people make a sudden profit through a miraculous set of circumstances which could only have come about through God's own direction. Yet immediately they start worrying, "What will I live on afterwards?"

We have to develop our trust and not worry from one to day to the next. Someone who worries what he is going to eat tomorrow lacks faith. God brings each person his livelihood in such a way that it is always a test. The main thing is to lift our eyes upwards each time we need something. There is no other way except to search for God in the remote places. For, "Those who seek the Lord will lack nothing good" (Psalms 34:11).

The Locust's Antenna

Rabbi Zeira found Rabbi Yehudah standing in the entrance of his father-in-law's house. He saw that he was in a humorous mood and would give him the answer to anything he might ask about all the different phenomena in the world. [Rabbi Zeira] asked, "Why is the antenna of the locust soft?" [Rabbi Yehudah answered,] "Because it lives in the willow, and if its antenna were hard it would snap when it hits the wood, blinding the locust—because as Rabbi Shmuel taught, the locust's vision depends on its antenna."

(*Shabbat* 77b; see *Rashi*, ad loc.)

The teaching of *Ayeh?* is founded on the deepest Torah concepts about God's relation to the universe. We live in a world where Godliness is often invisible—to the point that some philosophers have tried to deny God altogether. Quite ordinary people also find themselves troubled by doubts at one time or another. Rebbe Nachman was well aware of the anguish such thoughts may produce. His answer is as daring as it is awesome. Rebbe Nachman taught:

"God created the universe for the sake of His lovingkindness, because he wanted to *reveal* His lovingkindness, and were it not for the creation of the universe, to whom would He show it? Therefore He brought about the entire Creation, from the beginning of *Atzilut*, the World of Emanation, to the central point of the physical world—all in order to display His lovingkindness.

"But when God wanted to create the universe, there was no place to create it, because everything was infinite, while the universe necessarily had to be finite. Therefore He contracted His Infinite Light to the sides, and through this contraction, the *Chalal HaPanui*, Vacated Space, was formed. It was in this Vacated Space that all the "days" and all the Divine qualities were manifest, making up the creation of the world.

"The Vacated Space was essential for the creation of the universe, because without it there would have been no place for the universe to be created. Yet the contraction through which the Vacated Space came about is impossible to comprehend with human reason; only in time to come will the mystery be unraveled. It is impossible to comprehend because we have to make two contradictory statements about it: *yesh* and *ayin*. Since the Vacated Space came about through the contraction, with God removing, as it were, His Godliness from there, we have to say there is no Godliness there (*ayin*). Otherwise it would not be empty and all would be Infinite Light, with no room for the creation of the universe. On the other hand, the truth is that Godliness must certainly be present (*yesh*), because nothing can exist without God's life force. It is this contradiction which makes it impossible to comprehend the Vacated Space until the future time" (*Likutey Moharan* I, 64).

Because the Vacated Space is apparently devoid of Godliness, it is the source of all the philosophical problems that seem to raise doubts about God. And precisely because of the concealment of Godliness there, it seems as if there is no solution to these problems. This was why Rebbe Nachman warned us not to get involved with them at all, since "all who go into her will not return" (Proverbs 2:19). In these matters, we must rely on faith alone.

The Kabbalists symbolized the Vacated Space as a locust "whose clothing is of it and in it" (*Bereshit Rabbah* 21:5). The "clothing" refers to the contractions involved in the creation of the Vacated Space. Through these garments, it is possible to understand that it is of Him and in Him (see *Likutey Moharan*, loc. cit. 6).

In the following excerpt (*Likutey Halakhot, Hilkhot Eruvey Techumin* 6:8-10). Reb Noson relates Rebbe Nachman's teachings about the Vacated Space to *Ayeh?* in order to elucidate the questions Rabbi Zeira asked Rabbi Yehudah when the latter was in a humorous mood.

Reb Noson writes:

Only from *Ayeh?*, the Hidden Utterance of *Bereshit*, can the places removed from holiness receive their life force. This is because of the very concealment and mystery of *Ayeh?* These places cannot receive their vitality from God's revealed glory, because, "I will not give My glory to another," and these places constitute the *Sitra Achra*, the "*Other* Side."

What are these "places removed from holiness"? They are not necessarily *physical* places (though there certainly are places that are evil). Mostly, we experience them as *mental* places—states of mind we encounter at certain times in our lives, as when we are confronted with baffling doubts that seem to contradict the most basic tenets of faith. Sometimes they involve philosophical conundrums that seem to go on and on without end. What is the source of such doubts? Rebbe Nachman taught that they derive from the Vacated Space (see *Likutey Moharan* I, 64, quoted above).

Ayeh? involves the mystery of the Vacated Space, formed as it was through the concealment of Godliness. The "filthy places" that are cut off from holiness appear to be devoid of Godliness, because Godliness is concealed in such places—God's glory cannot be revealed there. However, *Ayeh?* teaches that even in these places, Godliness *must* be present, albeit concealed. Thus the main solution for anyone who has fallen there is to search for God. And it is impossible to find Him through reason or logic, only with faith, through pleading and searching *Ayeh?*—"*Where* is the place of His glory?"

Understand the practical implications of this lesson, because it can help and support you no matter what you encounter in life. You never know what may happen to you. Anyone who genuinely wants to enter the paths of holiness is tested by being thrown into places like these. If you practice the teaching of *Ayeh?* you will be able to turn your falls into great ascents. But it takes tremendous determination to succeed. The main thing is to know the limitations of the human mind, "for I am more a brute than a man" (Proverbs 30:2). You can succeed only by putting aside your own ideas completely and relying on faith. You must have faith in the teachings of the Tzaddikim, that Godly vitality is present in the most remote places, even in the "filthy places." Using human intelligence, it is impossible to find God's glory there, because these places are apparently "devoid of Godliness." But if you have faith and search *Ayeh?*, you can rise to the greatest heights.

This will help us understand Rabbi Zeira's question and Rabbi Yehudah's answer. The locust is a reference to the Vacated Space, as we saw above. The antenna (Hebrew: *keren*) alludes to the Godly vitality channeled there under a veil of the greatest concealment. The word *keren* (literally, horn) suggests the strength or power of an animal or human. The strength of an ox and other beasts is manifested in the horns, and the term is also used to refer to human strength, as in, "His horns are the horns of the buffalo" (Deuteronomy 33:17) and, "I will break all the horns of the wicked, while the horn of the Tzaddik will be exalted" (Psalms 75:11), which means that the power of the wicked will be broken and the Tzaddik will prevail. (Also see Amos 6:13, I Samuel 2:10, Psalms 148:14, etc.) The source of a creature's strength depends on the Godly vitality which is channeled to that creature, whether by holy or unholy means. Thus, the manifestation of Godly vitality is also termed *KeReN* (cf. Habakkuk 3:4: "and a brightness appears as the light; He has rays [*KaRNaim*] at His side," and Exodus 34:35: "the skin of the face of Moses beamed [*KaRaN*] with light").

Rabbi Zeira asked why the antenna of the locust is *soft*. In other words, why is the vitality of the Vacated Space "soft" in the sense that no Godly light is visible there? The animating vitality is finer than fine, being hidden from all who enter, just as something soft and pliant is swept aside by all. Rabbi Yehudah answered, "Because it lives in the willow." The willow, a plant which has neither taste nor smell, symbolizes those who are removed from holiness. Thus the Rabbis compared Jewish sinners to the willow (*Vayikra Rabbah* 30:12). Rabbi Yehudah continued, "Because if it were hard it would snap when it hits the wood." He implied that in these remote places, the key to standing firm is precisely by being soft. "Let be (Hebrew: *haRPu*—literally, make soft) and know that I am God" (Psalms 46:11). This is connected with the saying of the Rabbis, "A person should always be soft like a reed and not hard like a cedar" (*Ta'anit* 20b). All the winds in the world cannot move a reed from its place because it is soft and pliant and always yields. Yet it is firm and strong at the root, which is why the winds cannot pull it up. Not so with the hard cedar.

The remote places are the embodiment of the Vacated Space. One feels tormented with doubts, material desires and all kinds of problems. Rabbi Yehudah was saying: Don't start with questions (*KuShiot*) and answers. "Do not harden (*taKShu*) your hearts" (Psalms 95:8). In these situations, the way to remain steadfast is by being soft as a reed, not reacting to any of the questions and problems that plague you. Everyone has to face opposition from the outside and confusion from within. Don't try to answer back. "I am like a person who does not hear, with no defenses on his lips" (Psalms 38:14). There is no answer to the problems and difficulties arising from this source. Where you should remain firm, however, is in your *faith*, like a soft reed that is firmly rooted under the water, even if it seems pliant and yielding above.

Be strong in the traditional faith handed down from our ancestors. Pay no attention to all the distracting problems stemming from the "filthy places," and don't try to solve them even if it seems as if you are yielding. King David was the Messianic king whose role was to rectify the remote places and lift up all who have fallen there. When he was anointed king, he said, "I am this day *soft* and just anointed king" (II Samuel 3:39)—soft as a reed, because only the Mashiach attains this quality perfectly so as to conquer the whole world.

Rabbi Yehudah continued: "If its antenna were hard it would snap when it hits the wood, blinding the locust." In the remote places, the light is very concealed. One who is hard and stubborn, involving himself in every problem and searching for solutions, will end up being blinded. His eyes will become closed like those of a blind man, because these problems have no solution. The only solution is to be soft as a reed, answering nothing, firm at the roots—the roots of faith—searching and entreating *Ayeh?* This is the way to rise up. There is much more to explain about how to be soft, but it is impossible to put it in writing. Anyone with intelligence and a genuine desire for the truth will understand for himself.

Ayeh? and *Azamra!*

The previous sections elucidated some of the many aspects of *Ayeh?* as they apply to different facets of life. Essentially, they all point in one direction: the need to search for God when we are low. *Ayeh?* is the highway leading from alienation and depression to happiness and joy. As such, it is the fitting sequel to *Azamra!*, Rebbe Nachman's path to happiness via looking for the good points in ourselves and others. The two lessons go hand in hand, each complementing and completing the other. They are the fundamental pillars of Rebbe Nachman's path in life.

In the following excerpt (*Likutey Halakhot, Hilkhot Eruvey Techumin* 6:1-3, 5-7, 20-23, 28-30), Reb Noson discusses *Azamra!* and *Ayeh?* together, explaining how each is necessary in different phases of our spiritual journey. He anchors his analysis on the concept of Shabbat, because Shabbat is the root of all our joy and holiness. Reb Noson bases his discussion on the concept of the Shabbat *techum*, the Shabbat boundary. Halakhically, this is a spatial concept referring to the limits within which a person may travel on Shabbat. Reb Noson expands the spiritual dimension of the concept of *techum*, showing how it signifies the protective boundary that guards our Jewish identity. *Azamra!* and *Ayeh?* comprise the "boundary" that keeps us within the realm of holiness and joy throughout all the challenges of life. These two teachings serve as the remedy for the two main flaws in the Creation, the Vacated Space and the Shattering of the Vessels.

Not only does Reb Noson's discussion demonstrate the great depth of *Azamra!* and *Ayeh?*, but it also offers a profound and inspiring insight into the meaning of Shabbat, revealing the power of Shabbat to bring holiness and joy into our lives every day and every moment.

Reb Noson writes:

The holiness of the Jewish People is rooted in the holiness of Shabbat, which encompasses the entire Torah. All the holiness of the Jewish People—whether the holiness that comes from Torah study or from keeping the mitzvot—is itself the holiness of Shabbat. And this holiness is not confined to the day of Shabbat alone. We must also draw it into our lives on the six working days as well. "*Remember* the Shabbat day to sanctify it" (Exodus 20:8)—this implies, "Remember it from Sunday onwards" (*Beitzah* 16b). We remember the Shabbat on weekdays by observing the Torah and mitzvot day by day. Through them, we fill ourselves with the holiness of Shabbat.

Clearly, then, it is of utmost importance to honor the Shabbat. The main thing is to celebrate the Shabbat day joyously and wholeheartedly. We should banish all worry and depression from our minds, and even sadness over our various failings. On weekdays, too, we should keep well away from depression, especially when we are engaged in something like Torah study and mitzvah performance. Especially then, we should forget our worries about our sins. We should just take joy in the little good we still have in us. This certainly applies on Shabbat. On that day, there should be no sadness or depression at all.

The essence of the holiness of Shabbat lies in putting all our energies into being happy, because Shabbat is a day of joy in all the worlds. On that day, all the different ways of achieving happiness and joy shine with a special glow. It is still up to us to put them into practice. But on Shabbat it is much easier to do so, and by striving for happiness on Shabbat we can achieve it on the six working days as well. The key to holiness, then, is to bring the joy of Shabbat into the six working days, investing the weekday mitzvot with joy—Shabbat joy. This joy completes the mitzvah and causes it to ascend to the upper worlds.

Rebbe Nachman's writings are filled with ideas for achieving a constant state of happiness so that nothing gets you down (see *Advice*, Joy). Being happy is the foundation of everything else. But the two most basic methods can be found in the lessons of *Azamra!* and

Ayeh? Ayeh? is the subject of this book. The main idea of *Azamra!* is that even someone who feels very far from God and full of failings should nevertheless look for his good points. It is simply not possible that he never did anything worthwhile in his life. These good points will bring him to genuine happiness. It is vital to follow these teachings because they are the basis of Jewish living, as anyone who desires to be a true Jew knows well. But the only way to succeed is by drawing on the power of Shabbat and the power of the true Tzaddikim. Indeed, the holiness of Shabbat is the holiness achieved by the Tzaddik, as indicated in the *Zohar*: "You are the Shabbat of all the days" (*Zohar* III, 144b).

On Shabbat, the approach of *Azamra!* truly shines. To a certain extent, the forces of evil always have the six working days in their grasp. They even have a grip on the good we do, which is why our mitzvot are so often accompanied by a kind of heaviness (see *Likutey Moharan* I, 139 and 277). The forces of evil grasp onto the "feet" of each mitzvah, as alluded to in the verse, "her [the Shekhinah's] *feet* go down to death" (Proverbs 5:5). Weighted down, the mitzvah cannot go forth and show itself before God in full pride. But when Shabbat comes, the "feet" are released from the hold of evil. Thus it is written, "If you turn away your *foot* because of the Shabbat" (Isaiah 58:13). On Shabbat, the mitzvah can go before God, and He is delighted. Even if the mitzvah was done in a very modest way, God's love for Israel, His special People, is so strong that He takes great delight in each mitzvah and converts it into an open pathway towards Him.

On the six working days, the grip of darkness is so strong that it takes a tremendous effort to sift out the good from the mitzvot that we do. We have to work hard to remind ourselves of all the good points our mitzvot contain, and try not to be discouraged by the inadequate way we feel we perform them. Often we are assailed by all kinds of dark thoughts about our failure to live up to our ideals, not to mention our actual sins. Sometimes we are so dragged down that we come to believe there is no hope at all. All this is the work of the Evil One. It has nothing to do with genuine modesty—the Evil One is trying to pull us down completely. That is why it is so hard to remember our good points. Thank God, we do receive help in the most wonderful, roundabout ways to follow the path of *Azamra!* Our ability to prevail derives from the power of Shabbat. By bringing the holiness of Shabbat into each of the six working days, we acquire the strength to follow the path of *Azamra!*

On Shabbat, the path of *Azamra!* radiates perfectly, because then the influence of the forces of evil vanishes along with depression and sadness. "All the forces of anger and severity flee, and there is no other power besides God in all the worlds" (Zohar II, 135b). Shabbat brings an awakening of infinite forces of love and kindness. The ways of God—His true kindnesses—are revealed and shine in all the worlds. For God does not look at a person's evil, only at the good in him. "He did not see sin in Jacob" (Numbers 23:21). On Shabbat, all the mitzvot of the Jewish People begin to go before God in pride because the forces of evil, sadness and depression that exerted a grip on their "feet" vanish, revealing the precious holiness of all the good points of the mitzvot. Then these mitzvot go before God in pride, opening the way for everyone to come close to Him. On Shabbat, the way of *Azamra!* is clear and radiant, because the forces of evil are powerless to conceal good beneath a layer of bad. Therefore, only the good shines forth—the good points of all the mitzvot—until evil and depression fall away completely and song and praise break forth: "A psalm, a *song* for the Shabbat day" (Psalms 92:1). "The Shabbat day praises and sings" (Shabbat Morning Liturgy). From the gathering of all the good points in the mitzvot carried out by every Jew— even Jewish sinners—the most amazing songs and praises are formed. "I will praise God with my life; I will sing to my God with the little I have left" (Psalms 146:2, as explained in *Azamra!*).

The essence of the teaching of *Ayeh?* in all its subtlety and depth also derives from the holiness of Shabbat and the holiness of the true Tzaddikim. The Tzaddikim are those who have already attained the level of *Ayeh?* in holiness as a result of their spiritual achievements. They have climbed level by level until they have reached the ultimate heights of *Ayeh?*, which is the Supreme Crown, *Bereshit*. And through their own success, they acquire the power to lighten the way for others, even those who have fallen to the "filthy places." If those who have fallen will only search *Ayeh?*—"*Where* is the place of His glory?"—they, too, can reach the heights of *Bereshit*, the Hidden Utterance.

This power of the Tzaddikim is itself the power of the holiness of Shabbat. For on Shabbat all the souls and all the worlds rise up to the level of *Ayeh?*, which is the Will of Wills, the highest source of the Creation. Through the power of the holy Shabbat, when the level of *Ayeh?* radiates in holiness, and through the power of the true Tzaddikim, who reached *Ayeh?* in holiness, it is possible to give new life to all who have fallen to the "filthy places." Then they, too, can raise themselves up by virtue of the fact that they did not despair, even in the situation in which they found themselves. Instead of giving up, they must search for a way to return to God.

The connection between *Ayeh?* and Shabbat illuminates what the Rabbis said about Adam's sin and his banishment from the Garden of Eden: "the Shabbat protected him" (*Zohar* II, 138a). Adam's sin encompasses all the sins in the world. Shabbat serves as the main defense and the means of escape—because it is from Shabbat that these paths derive, giving us the means to return to God and make amends.

• The Shabbat Boundary—Two Alephs

The law of the Shabbat *techum* permits a person to walk a maximum of two thousand cubits from the edge of the town in which he spends Shabbat. These two thousand cubits are called the Shabbat boundary. It is forbidden to travel any further, as it is written, "Let no man go out of his place" (Exodus 16:29).

(See *Shulchan Arukh, Orach Chaim* 397)

The Hebrew word for "thousand," *ELePh*, has the same letters as *ALePh*, the first letter of the Hebrew alphabet. In Kabbalistic literature, the letter aleph signifies *seichel*, intellect or wisdom. Thus the *two thousand* cubits of the Shabbat boundary suggest two alephs, two wisdoms, like the "two thousand years by which the Torah preceded the world" (*Pesachim* 54a). These two wisdoms are the two paths of *Azamra!* and *Ayeh?* that comprise the boundary of holiness, the protective limit that has the power to keep us within the bounds of Jewish sanctity all our lives. (We have seen above that Shabbat encompasses the entire holiness of the Jewish People.)

Azamra! is one aleph. It is written, "The *thousand* are for you, Shlomo" (Song of Songs 8:12). *ShLoMo* alludes to Shabbat, being "the king of peace (*ShaLoM*)" (see Rashi on Song of Songs 1:1). According to the Kabbalah, the added spirituality of Shabbat causes a *thousand* lights to shine forth on the Jewish People. All this light is channeled down through the path of *Azamra!* by means of the true Tzaddikim, who judge everyone positively and find good points in every single Jew, down to the lowest. The Tzaddikim teach this path to all the people, so that each individual can find his own good points and all can return to God. The positive point is "an angel, an intercessor, one out of a *thousand*, to vouch for a man's uprightness" (Job 33:23). Even if we only find one good point in a thousand, or even if in the positive merit itself the good is only one part out of a thousand, it still helps. This is the lesson the Rabbis learned from the above verse. They said, "Even if that very angel contains nine hundred and ninety-nine parts for the prosecution and only one part for the defense, the accused person is still saved" (Shabbat 32a). In other words, even if our mitzvot or our positive points contain only a fraction of good, they still have the power to move us onto the scale of merit so that we can attain the thousand lights that radiate on Shabbat.

The path of *Ayeh?* is also an aleph. The letter aleph alludes to the level of *Ayeh?*, the Hidden Utterance of *Bereshit*, since *Ayeh?* is the *Pele*, Sublime Wonder (*PeLE* has the same Hebrew letters as *ALePh*). This is the level of Keter, of which the Rabbis said, "What is too wondrous (*muPhLA*) for you, do not inquire into" (Chagigah 13a). Of this level it is said, "Telling the end from the beginning (*reishit*)" (Isaiah 46:10)—alluding to *Bereshit*. As we have seen, on Shabbat the light of *Ayeh?* radiates in an awesome, wondrous manner. This is the source of the perceptions of the true Tzaddik; by rising to the level of *Ayeh?* he has the power to bring home to all the Jewish People that even a person who has fallen to the most remote places can still search for God even there, and through searching *Ayeh?* he can rise to the highest levels. Thus we see that *Ayeh?* is also an aleph that radiates with a special light on Shabbat.

These two alephs comprise the Shabbat boundary because these two paths keep a Jew within the bounds of holiness, as signified by the two thousand cubits of the Shabbat techum. The measurement of the Shabbat *techum* is derived from the laws concerning the cities of the Levites (Numbers 35:2ff.). These cities were surrounded by one thousand cubits of open land and an additional one thousand cubits of fields and vineyards. The Kohanim (priests) and the Levites symbolize the Tzaddikim in each generation and their followers, respectively. The true Tzaddik is the Kohen, as the Rabbis taught on the verse, "The lips of the Kohen keep knowledge, and they should seek the law at his mouth, for he is a messenger (*MaLACh*) of the Lord of Hosts" (Malachi 2:7). The Rabbis commented: "If he is like an angel (*MaLACh*) of God"—in other words, if he is saintly—"then they should seek the law at his mouth" (Moed Katan 17a). Thus, the Kohen is equated with the Tzaddik. As for the Levites, their role was to be "joined with and minister to" the priests (Numbers 18:2)—just as the followers of the Tzaddik are attached to him and carry out his projects. The Levites received guidance and teaching from the Kohanim in order to give direction to the Jewish People.

Forty-eight cities were apportioned to the Kohanim and the Levites—six cities of refuge for those guilty of manslaughter, and an additional forty-two cities of their own. The number of cities alludes to the fundamentals of Jewish belief, as contained in the *six* words of the verse "*Shema Yisrael*" (Deuteronomy 6:4) and the *forty-two* words of the ensuing paragraph beginning, "*Ve-ahavta*—And you shall love" (ibid.,

6:5-9). The whole task of the Tzaddikim and their followers is to instill perfect faith in the Jewish People, for that is the whole Torah.

All forty-eight cities possessed two thousand cubits of common land, fields and vineyards; from this measurement, the Shabbat boundary is derived. This connects with the work of the Tzaddikim to instill in the Jewish People the twin approaches of *Azamra!* and *Ayeh?* so that no Jew will go beyond the bounds of holiness. The thousand (*ELePh*) cubits of open land had to be completely *empty* (see *Rashi* on Numbers 35:2), which connects with the concept of *Ayeh?*—itself an *ALePh*. For *Ayeh?* is the concealed life source of the remote places and is equated with the Vacated Space, as we have seen.

The second thousand (*ELePh*) cubits of fields and vineyards allude to the path of *Azamra!*, also an *ALePh*. By finding the good points in the Jewish People and bringing them back to God, we sow fields and plant vineyards (cf. Psalms 107:37: "they sowed fields and planted vineyards and they brought forth fruits and produce"). All the good that the Tzaddikim uncover in the Jews produces fruits in the Supernal Field, where Israel's work in sowing and planting lies. It is customary to recite Psalm 107 on the eve of Shabbat; its description of all the trials and tribulations of the Jewish People corresponds to the suffering of the soul on the six working days (see *Rebbe Nachman's Wisdom* #270). To wit: "They wandered in the wilderness" (v. 4), "They cried out to God" (v. 6), "Those who dwelled in darkness in the shadow of death" (v. 10), and, "They will thank God for His kindness and wonders" (v. 15). All God's wonders in saving us from evil to keep us firm are performed through the power of the Tzaddikim, who strengthen us with these two holy paths rooted in the spiritual power of Shabbat. Therefore we recite this Psalm as Shabbat begins, concluding with the words, "He turns the desert into a pool of water" (v. 35), and, "they sowed fields and planted vineyards" (v. 37).

• Refinement of the Creation

God placed man in a world in which good and evil are intermingled, to give him the opportunity to sift out the good and earn the reward of the World to Come. The work of sifting and refining is carried out on the six weekdays through the thirty-nine categories of labor, travel, and so on.

The thirty-nine categories of labor are the paradigm for all labor. Since they were all necessary for the building of the Sanctuary—itself the model of perfection—they are the means through which the entire creation is refined. Shabbat, however, is not the time for the work of refinement. Shabbat is on a plane *beyond* this world; therefore, the thirty-nine categories of labor are forbidden on Shabbat and we refrain from travel. The weekday work of refining the Creation, sifting the good from the bad, finding the sparks of holiness and raising them up from the forces of evil, is accomplished by the great Tzaddikim and their followers, mainly through the twin paths of *Azamra!* and *Ayeh?*

There are two broad divisions among the forces of evil. The first division includes those forces that derive from the Shattering of the Vessels. God's Infinite Light could not be received by man in its initial intensity. The vessels designed to hold that Light broke, causing good to be mixed up with evil and giving man freedom of choice. The Shattering of the Vessels projected sparks of holiness, so that even in the darkest and most remote places, there is some good to be found. The second division includes the forces of evil that derive from the Vacated Space, which is devoid of Godliness and where God cannot be found by reason at all, only through faith (see above, p. 53). The Vacated Space is not only the source of the intractable problems of philosophy, but also of the temptations and allurements of evil, which are themselves rooted in godlessness.

In essence, the work of refinement is accomplished through *teshuvah* and good deeds. Adam's sin threw numerous holy sparks among the forces of evil, and the same happens whenever anyone sins. The mind of the sinner becomes encumbered with all kinds of confusions and negative ideas, to the point that his thoughts and ideas may come down to him from the level of the Vacated Space itself, which is the source of all the "filthy places."

The only way for a sinner to rise up from there is through the twin paths of *Azamra!* and *Ayeh?* Through *Azamra!* he can sift out the good from the forces of evil that derive from the Shattering of the Vessels. Much good is mixed up among the evil here, and it must be refined. This is accomplished by the true Tzaddikim and their followers through the teaching of *Azamra!* But there is an even more powerful level of evil rooted in the Vacated Space. When negative thoughts and confusions derive from there, the only remedy is to search *Ayeh?*—"*Where* is the place of His glory?"

The work of refinement on the six weekdays is accomplished through the twin approaches of *Azamra!* and *Ayeh?* But because of the powerful grip of evil on the six weekdays, hard work and effort are needed in the form of the thirty-nine categories of labor, travel, and so on. Even then, the ability to accomplish this work derives from the holiness of Shabbat. Although the work of refinement ceases on Shabbat, the weekday work can only succeed through the power of the holiness of Shabbat. Likewise, the *tikkun*, rectification, which is the goal of all the work of refinement is not complete until Shabbat. Only then does the refined holiness go back up to its place. When Shabbat commences, all the sparks of holiness that were sifted and refined on the six working days rise upwards. (All this is discussed in mystical terms in the writings of the Kabbalists; the present discussion aims to give practical help to the individual in his efforts to come close to God in his actual situation.)

On Shabbat it is forbidden to travel beyond the two thousand cubits of the Shabbat boundary because this day is not the time for the work of refining. Rather, it is a time of great lovingkindness, when only the good of the Jewish People radiates. "I am black but beautiful" (Song of Songs 1:5). "I am black—on the six working days—but beautiful—on the Shabbat" (*Shir HaShirim Rabbah* 1:5). This is the idea of *Azamra! Ayeh?* also radiates on Shabbat, as we have seen. Together these two paths make up the two *ALePhs*, two *ELePhs*, adding up to the two thousand cubits of the Shabbat boundary. One is permitted to journey only *within* the limit—that is, within the framework of these two paths.

• *Eruvey Techumin*—Mixing the Limits

If someone knows he will have to travel beyond the Shabbat *techum* for a mitzvah or some other pressing purpose, the Halakhah offers him two possibilities.

These are known as *eruvey techumin*, mixing the limits. The first method is as follows: Before sundown on Friday, one travels to the edge of the Shabbat techum, as measured from the place where he lives, and sits there until dark. Wherever a person is during the twilight period, this is where he acquires his "Shabbat residence" for that Shabbat, and it is from there that his Shabbat boundary is measured. This individual, having acquired two thousand cubits in all directions from the place where he sat at sundown, can still go back to his home, because it is within two thousand cubits from there. But he can also go two thousand cubits in the opposite direction. In effect, he has created a boundary of four thousand cubits from his home.

The second method of mixing the limits is related to the Shabbat *food*. Prior to Shabbat, one leaves enough food for two Shabbat meals at the edge of the Shabbat techum, as measured from his home. Having done this, his Shabbat boundary is now measured *from the place of the food*, again giving him a boundary of four thousand cubits from his home (Shulchan Arukh, Orach Chaim 408).

Why can the Shabbat boundary be measured from the place where *food* is left? The answer relates to the fact that the work of refinement on the six weekdays, with all the labor and traveling it involves, is primarily concerned with livelihood and food. For, "All a person's work is for his mouth" (Ecclesiastes 6:7). The task of refinement became necessary because of sin. The source of all sin is Adam's sin, which involved eating. After Adam ate from the Tree of Knowledge of Good and Evil, God decreed, "In toil you shall eat…with the sweat of your brow you shall eat bread" (Genesis 3:17-19). All the efforts involved in the thirty-nine categories of labor and travel result from this decree. One must invest these efforts to sift out the sparks of good from amidst the two divisions of the forces of evil. This is accomplished through the two approaches of *Azamra!* and *Ayeh?*

On weekdays, one must exert much effort to eat in holiness because of the hold of evil. Therefore, it is not good to eat excessively during the week. On Shabbat, however, the act of eating is entirely holy (cf. *Likutey Moharan* I, 57 and 276). On Shabbat, the two approaches of *Azamra!* and *Ayeh?* radiate with a special light, rendering the forces of evil powerless. Since eating on Shabbat is holy, it is a mitzvah to eat plentifully on that day. (Obviously, this does not mean overindulging.) Eating plentifully on Shabbat lends added radiance to the two paths of *Azamra!* and *Ayeh?* As the Rabbis said, "Chew with your teeth and you'll get strength in your *feet*" (*Shabbat* 152a)—the "feet" allude to these two paths. Eating is the main channel for Shabbat joy. The Rabbis said that nothing is better for a person than to eat, drink and be happy on Shabbat and Yom Tov (cf. *Yerushalmi, Shabbat* 15:3). The joy of Shabbat gives radiance to the twin paths of *Azamra!* and *Ayeh?* This is why the Shabbat boundary of two thousand cubits, alluding to the two alephs of *Azamra!* and *Ayeh?*, begins from the place where the Shabbat food is left.

• Unification

To explain more deeply: The fundamental rectification of all the worlds is accomplished by connecting and unifying all the revealed Utterances within the Hidden Utterance, from which they all derive. This is brought about through eating in holiness—eating on Shabbat. Eating connects body and soul, which is the concept of connecting and unifying all the worlds with God. Just as the soul animates and sustains the body, God animates and sustains all the worlds (cf. *Berakhot* 10a). Eating in holiness therefore brings about a great unification (cf. *Likutey Moharan* I, 62), because it epitomizes the unification that comes about when all the worlds are connected and unified with the root of their vitality—God, Who sustains them all. All the revealed Utterances are then included in the primordial point of the Creation, the Hidden Utterance of *Bereshit*.

The forces of evil draw their strength from the *disunity* that comes from not believing in God as the life force of all things. Precisely because the root of all things lies in the Hidden Utterance of *Ayeh?*, a place of great concealment that cannot be grasped intellectually at all, the forces of evil draw their life force from there. This is also the place from which all the philosophical notions of atheism stem, since it is truly impossible to understand through reason alone how all the worlds were created by and are governed by the Most Hidden. This understanding can only be achieved through faith. With faith, we pass *beyond* earthly reason and knowledge. (This is why the Jews are called *IVRim*, Hebrews, from the root word *EiVeR*, beyond).

Human logic ultimately leads to atheism, which derives from the Vacated Space and the Shattering of the Vessels. Even the forces of evil that derive from the Shattering of the Vessels are really rooted in the Vacated Space, which is the ultimate source of all the forces of evil. For had it not been for the initial contraction that brought about the Vacated Space, there would not have been the *ribui Or*, superabundance of Light, which caused the Vessels to shatter. Yet the Vacated Space was necessary in order for Creation to come about (see above, p. 50).

This explains why the fundamental *tikkun* is accomplished through *Ayeh?*—constantly searching for God. As soon as you *believe* that God is present, albeit concealed, even in the remote places that derive from the Vacated Space, then you can rise to the exalted level of *Ayeh?* itself, the Hidden Utterance of *Bereshit.* Then the vitality of these far-off places is bound once again to God, and all the Utterances are unified with their source in the Hidden Utterance. When the life force of evil is bound to the higher worlds, perfect unity is achieved. One accomplishes all this through eating in holiness.

Adam's sin of eating from the Tree of Knowledge brought death into the world, "for on the day you eat from it you will surely die" (Genesis 2:17). Death constitutes the separation of body and soul. Today it is impossible to refine the act of eating to such an extent that the body and soul are bound together in eternal life. Adam's sin caused a great deal of waste to become mixed up with food, and for this reason man is necessarily mortal. His mortality results from the blemish in eating: "With the sweat of your brow you will eat bread, until you return to the ground" (ibid., 3:19). The main *tikkun* after death comes about when the soul rises to the Hidden Utterance and returns to bring new life to the body so it can stand up at the Resurrection of the Dead and live forever.

The Tzaddik, however, nullifies his body and achieves an ascent to *Ayeh?* in his lifetime. Such a Tzaddik does not really die at all. His "death" is the ultimate in self-effacement, whereby he achieves a complete ascent to the Hidden Utterance in order to bring down new life to remedy all souls. Those who are not Tzaddikim must suffer pain in Gehinnom after death, in accordance with their deeds, to enable them to rise up. Everything is calculated justly. But even if a person fails to perfect himself during his lifetime, if he always tries to search for God, he gives himself a tremendous advantage. After death, when his soul passes through *Olam HaTohu*, the netherworld, he will be able to search for God even there, and will not be deceived. He will easily return to his resting place, all through the power of the true Tzaddik.

It requires constant effort throughout one's life to always sanctify one's eating, binding body and soul together in holiness, so that the eating itself brings about the unification of all the worlds with their source. One can attain this lofty goal by eating on Shabbat. On that day it is a great mitzvah to eat and enjoy, because eating on Shabbat is holy. The two paths of *Azamra!* and *Ayeh?* shine forth, and all the unifications are completed. All the worlds and all the Utterances are unified with their source in the Hidden Utterance, which then shines forth with a wonderful radiance.

Eruvey techumin, the mixing of the limits, is bound up with the Shabbat *meals* because the two thousand cubits of the Shabbat boundary—the two alephs of *Azamra!* and *Ayeh?*—derive their strength from the act of eating on Shabbat. The essence of the unification involves uniting the two alephs with each other. *Azamra!* is the *tikkun* for the Shattering of the Vessels, since it enables all the good—the sparks of holiness—to ascend to their place. These are the revealed Utterances, the source of all good, the Torah and mitzvot as a whole, that have the purpose of revealing God's glory until "the whole world is filled with his glory." But *Ayeh?*, which is the *tikkun* for the Vacated Space, is the *root* of the Torah and is higher than the Torah. The main thing is to join *Azamra!* and *Ayeh?* together in unity, binding the Torah as a whole, the revealed Utterances as expressed in all the worlds, with the supreme source, *Bereshit*, the Hidden Utterance. Then the two alephs are joined together, and this is the goal of eating in holiness (as explained in the writings of the ARI, *kavannot* of eating).

Eating on Shabbat accomplishes this unification because Shabbat is the time of rest and calm. On this day, one can think clearly and perceive with the eye of faith how everything is one—the whole world and all it contains have no life except from God, Who is hidden and concealed from all. This is the perfect unification. Such faith can only be achieved by drawing from the holiness of Shabbat, which is itself the holiness of the true Tzaddikim who have achieved a clear, tranquil perception. This is the true delight of the Shabbat rest, "a rest in peace and tranquility, quietude and trust" (from the Shabbat Afternoon *Amidah*). "In sitting still and rest shall you be saved, in quietness and confidence will be your strength" (Isaiah 30:15). This inner calm and tranquility cannot be communicated to anyone else; each one can only experience it for himself. It is something soft, like the antenna of the locust—soft as a reed, as it is written, "Let be and know that I am God" (Psalms 46:11). We can only follow our fathers and the holy Tzaddikim; in their merit, God will take pity on us and grant us a spark of His radiance.

• Abraham, Isaac and Jacob

"'And Jacob encamped before the city' (Genesis 33:18)—this teaches that he established the Shabbat boundary at sunset" (*Bereshit Rabbah, Vayishlach* 79:6).

The three Shabbat meals correspond to the three Patriarchs. The Friday night meal corresponds to Abraham, the man of lovingkindness, who judges everyone favorably and brings blessings of love upon the Jewish People through the good points he finds in them. This alludes to the path of *Azamra!* The Shabbat morning meal corresponds to Isaac, the "perfect offering," who asked *Ayeh?*—"*Where* is the lamb for the offering?" (Genesis 22:7). This alludes to the path of *Ayeh?*, which was established with the binding of Isaac. Isaac sweetens the severe judgments at their root. These judgments derive from the concealment of the Hidden Utterance; through *Ayeh?* they are sweetened.

Thus the first two Shabbat meals correspond to the first two Patriarchs and the two paths of *Azamra!* and *Ayeh?*, which are perfected by Shabbat eating. The third Patriarch, Jacob, is the "middle bar…passing through from end to end" (Exodus 26:28). Through Jacob, the two paths are joined together to form the perfect unity that comes about on Shabbat. This corresponds to *seudah shelishit*, the third Shabbat meal, which is the time of the Will of Wills (see above, p. 62). Then the Holy Ancient of Days reveals His Will. The rectification brought about by the two paths of *Azamra!* and *Ayeh?* is now perfect. This is why Shabbat is called "the inheritance of *Jacob*" (Isaiah 58:14). It is an inheritance without bounds, because all the forces limiting and oppressing holiness disappear and everything is brought back to God through the two paths of *Azamra!* and *Ayeh?*, unified as they are by Jacob, who opens them up to all. This underscores the significance of the teaching of the

Rabbis that Jacob established the Shabbat boundary of two thousand cubits, alluding to the two alephs of *Azamra!* and *Ayeh?*

• Two Are Better Than One

"Two are better than one...for if they fall, the one will lift up his fellow. ...And a threefold cord is not quickly broken" (Ecclesiastes 4:9-12).

"Two are better than one": These are the two paths of *Azamra!* and *Ayeh?*, which support a person at all times and keep him from falling in any way. "For if they fall, the one will lift up his fellow": Sometimes the way to hold ourselves is through the pathway of *Azamra!*, looking for the good points we still have in us. However, at times we cannot do even this and there seems to be no way to get out of our low. Then we have to hold ourselves with *Ayeh?*, searching for God in the very situation in which we find ourselves. *Ayeh?* is a path that is always open—no way in the world can the Evil One throw us off it. He may try to get it into our minds that all hope is lost because of our sins. But no matter what state we find ourselves in, the Rabbis teach that we can always search for God, even in the "filthy places," and so attain the ultimate heights of *Ayeh?* This way, we can always hold ourselves firm and strong until eventually God takes pity on us and opens our eyes to our good points. Then we will rejoice at God's saving power. "And a threefold cord is not quickly broken": This is Jacob, who joins the two paths together, bringing about the perfect *tikkun*.

Encouragement
Likutey Moharan II, 48

Rebbe Nachman taught:

When a person makes a start and tries to bring himself closer to God, he usually experiences a feeling of rejection. It is as if forces beyond his control deliberately want to prevent him from entering God's service. But in actual fact, this apparent rejection is nothing but a way of bringing him closer.

It takes tremendous determination not to get discouraged when you see that the days and years are passing by and despite all your efforts to bring yourself closer, you are still far away. You feel you have not even begun to enter the gates of holiness. You see how coarsely materialistic you still are, and how confused your mind still is. No matter what you try to do to serve God with something holy, it seems as if they will not let you. You begin to think that God is paying no attention whatsoever—as if He has no interest in your devotions. You keep calling out to Him, pleading with Him to help you. Yet you are still as far away as ever. You come to think that God is paying no attention because He does not want your devotions.

It takes tremendous determination to overcome all this. The key is to ignore all the efforts to discourage you. The truth is that all this apparent rejection has no other purpose than to bring you closer. All the Tzaddikim had to go through this, as we know from their personal testimony. They, too, felt that God had no interest in them, because they saw how long they had been searching, putting in hard work and effort, yet they were still far away. Had they not determinedly ignored these feelings, they would have remained where they were in the first place and would never have achieved what they did.

My friend and brother, the basic rule is to be firm and strong. Use all the strength you have to be persistent in your devotions. Pay no attention to all these discouraging thoughts. And if you are very far from God indeed and you feel your every movement must be a blemish in God's eyes, you should know that on the contrary, if someone were really all that coarse and materialistic, then even the slightest movement he makes to detach himself from his physicality and turn toward God is very great and precious. If he moves no more than a hairsbreadth in his efforts to purify himself and come closer, that hairsbreadth makes him run thousands and thousands of miles in the worlds above (see "The Melancholy Saint," *Rebbe Nachman's Stories* #16).

If you think about this, it will make you very happy. Indeed, you should make a great effort to always be happy, because depression does tremendous damage.

You should know that as soon as a person wants to start serving God, it is a very grave sin for him to be depressed. Depression comes from the Other Side, which God hates.

In order to serve God, you have to be *obstinate*. On no account should you yield and give up trying to do the few things you have started. Don't give up in any way, no matter what happens. Remember this well, because you will need it a great deal when you make a start in serving God. You must be very obstinate indeed, holding yourself strong and firm in your place each time they try to throw you down. This will happen very often. Your part is to carry on doing whatever you can and not let yourself fall completely, God forbid.

Inevitably, you will encounter all kinds of difficulties and setbacks. You will fall many times before you can enter the gates of holiness. Even the greatest Tzaddikim have experienced this. There are cases where a person is already at the gates of holiness, only to backslide because of these difficulties. When a person is close to the gates, the forces of evil try to prevent him from entering. This opposition pushes some people into a retreat. This is the way of the Evil One: When he sees a person literally next to the gates, he attacks more powerfully than ever. That is why you need to be so strong.

If you want to enter God's service, remember all this very well. Strengthen yourself every way you can and do what you can to continue with your devotions. Eventually you will surely succeed and enter the gates with God's help. God is overflowing with love, and He wants your devotions very much. You should know that every single effort counts. Every attempt you make to pull yourself even the slightest bit away from your materialism and towards spirituality are all added together. They will all come to help you when you really need it in times of pressure or trouble, God forbid.

Know: In life a person has to pass over a very narrow bridge. The main thing is not to be afraid.

I Have Strayed Like a Lost Sheep
Likutey Moharan I, 206

The main theme of *Ayeh?* is man's search for God. But there is also another aspect: God's search for man. We have to ask God to look for us and bring us back to Him, so that we do not stray off the track completely. This is Rebbe Nachman's teaching on the verse, "I have strayed like a lost sheep; seek out Your servant, for I have not forgotten Your mitzvot" (Psalms 119:176).

When a person commits a sin, it makes a big difference if he comes to his senses at once and repents. Then it will be easy for him to return to his place, because he has not yet strayed very far from the path of good. When a person sins, it means he turns aside from the upright path to travel a different path, a devious path. Branching off from it are any number of wrong turnoffs that lead deeper and deeper into error and corruption. As soon as one sets out on the wrong path, he goes further and further astray, becoming more and more entangled in these paths, until it is very hard for him to turn back.

God's way is to call to a person the moment He sees him straying from the path of good sense. He calls to him to turn back. He calls each person in the way most suited to him. Some He beckons with a hint. To others the summons is literally a cry. Some people kick and He has to strike them in order to call them. For the Torah cries out before them, "Fools! How long will you love foolishness?" (Proverbs 1:22) (*Zohar, Shemini* 36a). The Torah is the voice of God Himself, calling and begging those who stray to return to Him.

As long as a person has not strayed far from the upright path, it is easy for him to come back, because he still recognizes the voice. Only a short time ago he was close to God and listened to His voice, the voice of the Torah. He has not yet forgotten it or strayed too far along those other, more devious and bewildering paths. That is why it is easy for him to return. It is like when a sheep strays from the path and the shepherd immediately calls it. As long as the sheep has not yet strayed too far, it still recognizes the shepherd's voice and immediately responds. But once the sheep strays very far from the path, it forgets the shepherd's voice and no longer recognizes his call. The shepherd also gives up looking, because such a long time has passed since the sheep went astray and became lost. In the same way, when a person spends a long time in bad ways and strays very far from the upright path into all those corrupt, devious, confused and confusing paths, it is hard for him to repent.

Sometimes a person goes so far along these devious, tangled paths that his very wandering brings him back close to the place where he was in the beginning. Only a small distance separates him from there. Then just an easy test will bring him back to his place. However, when God calls him and arranges the test, the person does not recognize the voice and feels no imperative to return to his place. This is the difference between those who are "young" and those who are "old." One who is still "youthful" and has not grown old in his sins can return more easily than one who is "aged," because he is still closer and has not forgotten the voice.

This is the meaning of the verse, "I have strayed like a lost sheep": I have strayed from the good path like a lost sheep that has strayed from the road. This is why I beg of You, "Seek out Your servant, because I have not forgotten your mitzvot." Hurry and search for me as long as I still remember the voice of the Torah and mitzvot. Hurry and search for me *immediately*, because I have not yet forgotten Your mitzvot; I still recognize the call of the mitzvot that make up the Torah. That is why I beg You to take pity on me and search me out quickly—as long as "I have not forgotten Your mitzvot" and still recognize the voice of the Torah. Because when a person grows old in his sins, God forbid, it is very hard for God to seek him out, seeing as he has already forgotten the voice of the Torah and no longer recognizes it.

Therefore we have to beg God to hurry and bring us back to Him as long as we have not completely forgotten the call of the Torah and the mitzvot. This was King David's prayer: "Seek out Your servant, for I have not forgotten Your mitzvot."

Rebbe Nachman told his followers to "turn the lessons into prayers" (Likutey Moharan II, 25). *His prescription acknowledged the integral relationship between prayer and study in the spiritual life of a Jew. With the Rebbe's encouragement, Reb Noson wrote extensive prayers based on the lessons in Likutey Moharan, which he collected and published in Likutey Tefilot. The following is Reb Noson's prayer to fulfill the teaching of Ayeh?*

Reb Noson's Prayer
Likutey Tefilot II, 12

Let me wander round the streets. Let me search in the open places for the One my soul loves. I looked for Him, but I did not find Him. Let me get up and go round the city. Let me go to the mountains. I will lift up my eyes and look out into the distance. I will look and search *Ayeh?*—Where is He? Where is the place of His glory? Where can I get guidance? I need a way of finding Him and knowing Him. Because for all my searching, I have not found Him. He has taken Himself away from me because of all my sins. I have gone round everywhere. I have searched in every direction. But still I have not found the remedy. Now I have come back in shame to search for You, God—now, in my time of sorrow.

It is very painful for me, very bitter. Painful and bitter. I am filled with confusion. Where did You go? Where did You turn when You hid Your face from me and put me into the hands of all my sins—sins more numerous than the sands of the sea? Isn't it because God is not within me that all these troubles have caught up with Me? All my sins have made my heart crooked; they have twisted my mind and my brain. I have been cast off into places that are completely remote from holiness, the "filthy places." My heart has become so twisted and confused. I am devastated. I am full of knots and tangles. There is no end to them. I no longer have the strength to bear it—bitter pain and torment! Woe for all the sins I have ever done! My heart is pounding with trepidation. I have no strength left; the light of my eyes is gone. My friends and those who love me stand back from my suffering; my near ones have distanced themselves from me. What shall I say? What can I say to justify myself? God has found out my sins time and time again. What right do I have to cry out yet again to the King?

• There Is No Despair

Master of the Universe, You have assured us time and time again that there is no giving up, ever. There is no despair. If so, then I still have the courage to spread out my hands to You and hope for Your love and graciousness. You are a God of amazing wonders. Perhaps…perhaps You will show me new wonders and find new ways, ways never seen or known or created before, to bring me back to You with all my heart, truly and sincerely. Grant me success in my search to find You. Let me find You soon, so that I can bring myself genuinely close to You. Help me—because I am relying on You.

Master of the World, the pain of my heart is worse than ever. Take me out of my distress. The pain is just too much—if I tried to describe it, no one would believe me. O Lord my God, Master of the World, my eyes turn to You, longing and hoping, because You know the truth. You know how utterly pitiful I am. Look on my affliction, because the pain and torment of my heart are just too much to bear. See my misery. All my insides are in turmoil; my heart is all confused. Bitter! Bitter!

Help me succeed! Help me to search for Your glory—to search in sincerity and truth until I really find You. Be gracious and show pity—the same pity You showed from afar in letting us know about this exalted teaching of *Ayeh?*, through which it is possible to find You even after falling to the lowest low. Even then, it is still possible to find You by searching *Ayeh?*— "Where?" *Where* are You? *Where* is my holiness, my purity? *Where* is my soul? My *nefesh*? My *ruach*? My *neshamah*? Where is the Lord God of our Fathers Who brought us out of the land of Egypt, the filthiest place on earth? Where is the God who brought us up from the sea? Where is the place of His glory? By searching like this, we can turn even the biggest downfall into a mighty rise—if only You will help us in Your lovingkindness to carry out all the details of this teaching in accordance with Your will and the will of Your true Tzaddikim, who revealed it after it was concealed for so long. This way we will be able to find

You at all times and transform all our failings into great successes.

By following this teaching, I will be able to get up and pull myself out of the "filthy places" I have sunk to because of all my sins. I will be able to rise way above and return to You genuinely and sincerely with all my heart, which is what You want for me! I will be able to bring myself close to Your great and holy glory.

• **For the Sake of Your Glory**

Help me to do everything for the sake of Your glory. Let me weigh my actions carefully and examine everything I plan to do to see if it is in accordance with Your will and can enhance Your glory. If so, let me do it promptly and efficiently. If it is not for the glory of God, let me simply not do it! Let me pay no regard whatsoever to myself or my own esteem and glory. Let me pay no regard to anything else in the world— my only intention should be to glorify Your Name and enhance Your honor, truly and genuinely, until I succeed, with Your love and help, to magnify, elevate, enhance and beautify Your glory in the world.

So, too, may all Your People, the House of Israel, serve You sincerely and in purity all the days of their lives and forever, without sophistication. Let us stop listening to our stubborn hearts. Let us stop following our own clever notions and our own mistaken ideas.

Let us turn all our thoughts and feelings to You alone—to keep, do and carry out all the words of Your Torah in love, truth, purity and simplicity, the way our holy ancestors always did. Let us quickly fulfill the desire You had in creating Your universe—to enhance Your glory. In the words of the prophet: "Everything that is called by My Name and that I have created for My glory—I have formed it, I have made it" (Isaiah 43:7). Through us, let each of the different portions of Your glory be revealed in all the different things that exist in the world. For everything was created through the Ten Utterances, which reveal and magnify Your glory throughout all the different portions of the Creation.

• You Search For Me

Please, God, let me be counted among the Tzaddikim who ensure the continued existence of this world which You created through Ten Utterances. Help me succeed. Be gracious to me. Do not let me fail. I have gone astray like a lost sheep. Search for Your servant—because if I don't succeed in searching for You the way I should, I beg of You, my Father, Lord and King, my God: *You* search for *me*! You are filled with love and awesome kindness. Work wonders with me and give me *life*. Search out Your flock of lost ones, abandoned and leaderless as we are. Search for me, rejected, cast-off and hated as I am.

Take pity on me, scarred and contemptible as I am. Release me from all my lowly impulses and desires. Save me from them and have pity on me! Have pity on me and on my little ones. Don't put me into the hands of my enemies. Don't abandon me to godlessness. Save my soul from death and my spirit from the dogs. Those who hate me are all around me. Save me from the quicksand and don't let me sink into the depths of the waters. Don't let me get swallowed up by the engulfing depths. Don't let the pit devour me. Answer me, God, because Your kindness is the true good. You are full of love—turn to me. Don't hide Your face from Your servant in my moment of pain and trouble. Hurry and give me an answer. See how my strength is failing. See how I sigh and groan. Help me! Help me! Save me! Redeem me! Show me Your kindness and give me *life*! Bring me back to You and lovingly grant me atonement and forgiveness for all my sins and transgressions, from my earliest youth until today, and especially my sins against the covenant.

Please, God, forgive me and grant me atonement for the multitude of bad thoughts I have ever had—whether I had them willfully and deliberately or unwittingly and against my will and control. Let me search for You sincerely and in truth to bring healing and atonement for all the crooked thoughts and feelings in my mind and heart—be they doubts about You or Your ways and attributes, or about Your Tzaddikim and Your pure and upright ones. Let all these thoughts be atoned for and rectified as if I had brought You *olah*-sacrifices, which come to atone for the doubts of the heart. Please, God, strengthen me with Your exalted holiness. Don't abandon me or stand far off.

• Awareness

Save me quickly, God of my salvation. Help me from now on to genuinely sanctify and purify myself, and let me feel You and be aware of Your Godliness always. Moment by moment, let me be fully conscious in my mind and my heart how the whole world is filled with Your glory and Your sovereignty rules over all. Let me practice what King David said: "I have put God before me constantly" (Psalms 16:8). Let me never forget You day or night, neither waking nor sleeping, whether I am sitting at home or going on my way, lying down or getting up. Whether I'm eating, drinking, standing, sitting…in every thought, word and action, in my every movement every minute of the day, let me find You and feel Your Godliness and power and control over me and over the entire world. Because, "'If a man hides himself in secret, will I not see him?' says the Lord. 'Do I not fill the heavens and the earth?'" (Jeremiah 23:24).

Ruler of everything! God of love! You are full of kindness and goodness all the time. Help me to succeed in coming genuinely close to You! Cleanse me and purify me from all the filth and dirt with which I have sullied my soul because of all the sins I ever committed. Raise me up from corruption to purity, from profanity to holiness. Take me out of my darkness and bring me to the light. Quickly fulfill Your promise: "From all your impurities and all your idols, I will cleanse you" (Ezekiel 36:25).

Help me keep having new and original Torah ideas all the time. Loving God, let they be true and genuine Torah ideas, and help me get over the preliminary mental confusion quickly. Help me overcome all the various obstacles against finding and developing new Torah ideas. Let my mind and my thoughts be bound up with the holy Torah constantly. Let the bond be so strong that it can never be shaken. That way, I will always be able to conceive new and fresh ideas, which is what You want. And the power of the holy Torah will go before me constantly and lead me on the path of truth and justice, day by day and moment by moment. Through me will the words of King Solomon be fulfilled: "When you walk, it will lead you; when you lie down, it will watch over you; and when you awaken, it will talk with you" (Proverbs 6:22).

Our Father, our King, reveal the glory of Your Kingship over us very soon. Shine forth and be exalted through us in the eyes of all the living. Take pity on Your great glory, profaned as it is among the nations because of all our sins. Bring us back to You with all our hearts so that we can raise up Your great and holy glory until it fills the entire world, and all that has the breath of life will give glory and splendor to Your Name. They will tell of Your Name throughout the world. They will speak of the glory of Your Kingship and tell of Your might.

Master of the Universe, rule over all the world in Your glory. Be exalted over all the earth in Your splendor. Shine forth in the radiance of Your might over all the inhabitants of the earth. Let everything You have made know that You made it and everything You created understand that You created it. Then all that has breath will declare: "The Lord God of Israel is King and His sovereignty rules over all." They will bless the Name of Your glory, which is exalted beyond all blessing and praise. Blessed is the Lord, God of Israel, who does great wonders alone. Blessed is the Name of His glory forever. His glory will fill all the earth. Amen. Amen.

Never Give Up!
Chayey Moharan #97

Once there was a very wealthy man. He had a shop attached to his home, filled with various kinds of merchandise. Thieves came and robbed him of his possessions, and he lost a large part of what he had. But he collected what remained and was able to put himself back on his feet. He purchased more stock and once again became a shopkeeper.

Thieves came again and robbed him of what was left of his previous wealth. But once again he gathered together the little he had left from his stock and from his wife's jewelry, and succeeded in getting back on his feet. He set up a store to provide himself and his household with a livelihood.

Again thieves came and robbed him, and he became so impoverished that his house was completely empty. He went out and collected a miserable sum, bought a few bits and pieces, and went around the villages like the poor peddlers who travel about with bundles of goods, needles, pipes and similar small items. He went from village to village, trading needles for chickens and eggs from the gentiles, and this was how he earned his family's bread.

One day he was on his way from the villages, carrying his little bit of stock and a few items of food, when he was attacked by a bandit. The bandit was riding a horse and traveling with two enormous bundles. He wanted to rob him. The man started weeping and pleading with the bandit, but the bandit paid no attention and robbed him of the little he had. The man was left without anything at all, and he wept and wept, feeling very bitter indeed. As if his previous troubles had not been enough when he had been stripped of his great wealth! Now even the meager livelihood he had left had been torn from him.

Meanwhile, he noticed that the bandit had fallen from his horse. He was trying to get up, but the horse was standing at his side, trampling his head with its hooves. The bandit fell back and died. The man went over to look, and saw that the bandit had fallen to the ground, dead. He opened the bandit's bundles, and there he found all the merchandise, wealth and possessions that had been stolen from him, from beginning to end. He returned to his house in peace and became rich again as before.

Reb Noson writes:

I myself did not hear this story directly from the Rebbe, but from others who heard it from him. Its full implications as intended by the Rebbe are certainly beyond my understanding. But this much I feel I do understand: The story offers tremendous encouragement to every single person. It does not matter what may happen to a person in his lifetime. They may rob and plunder him. Even the little he has left, with which he tries to revive himself, they may stalk and strip from him. It may happen again and again, countless times. Even so, he should never despair of God's mercy and kindness. He should just raise his eyes to Heaven each time and weep and cry out to God, pleading with Him to look upon his wretchedness and toil. Then, at the very end, the robber will suffer a fall he never gets up from, while his victim will get back all the holiness, all the devotions and all the good that were stolen from him. He will return to his wealth and eternal goodness.

Faith

Rebbe Nachman's Stories, Parable #19

There was once a poor man who earned a living by digging clay and selling it. Once while digging, he discovered a diamond that was obviously worth a great deal. He took it to an expert to ascertain its value. The expert said, "No one here will be able to afford such a jewel. Go to London, the capital, and there you will be able to sell it."

The man was so poor he could not afford to make the journey. He sold everything he had and went from door to door, collecting funds for the trip. Finally he had enough to take him as far as the sea. He then wanted to board a ship, but he did not have any money. He approached the captain of one of the ships and showed him his diamond. The captain immediately welcomed him aboard the ship with great honor, assuming that he was a very wealthy and trustworthy person. He gave the poor man a first-class cabin and treated him like a wealthy personage.

The poor man's cabin had a view of the sea. Every day he sat by his porthole, looking at his diamond and rejoicing. He was especially particular to admire his diamond during mealtimes, since eating in good spirits is highly beneficial for digestion.

One day, he sat down to eat with the diamond lying in front of him on the table, where he could see it and enjoy it. Sitting there, he dozed off. Meanwhile, the mess boy came and cleared off the table, shaking the tablecloth with its crumbs and the diamond into the sea. When the poor man awoke and realized what had happened, he almost went mad with grief. He knew the captain was a ruthless man who would not hesitate to kill him for his fare.

Having no other choice, he continued to act happy, as if nothing had happened. The captain would usually speak to him a few hours every day, and on this day, he put himself in good spirits, so that the captain was not aware that anything was wrong.

The captain said to him, "I want to buy a large quantity of wheat that I will be able to sell in London for a huge profit. But I am afraid that I will be accused of stealing from the king's treasury. Therefore, I will arrange for the wheat to be bought in your name. I will pay you well for your trouble."

The poor man agreed. As soon as they arrived in London, the captain died. The entire shipload of wheat was in the poor man's name, and it was worth many times more than the diamond.

Rebbe Nachman concluded, "The diamond did not belong to the poor man, and the proof is that he did not keep it. The wheat, however, did belong to him, and the proof is that he kept it. But he got what he deserved only because he *remained* happy."

I Will Sing!
Azamra!

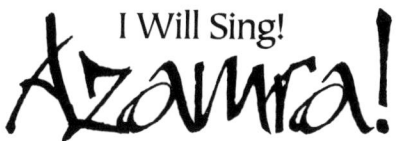
I Will Sing! Azamra!

REBBE NACHMAN

Published by
Breslov Research Institute
Jerusalem/New York

Copyright © 2023 BRESLOV RESEARCH INSTITUTE
ISBN 978-1-928822-09-7

Fourth edition

No part of this book may be translated, reproduced, stored in any retrieval system or transmitted, in any form or by any means, electronic, mechanical, photocopying, recording or otherwise, without prior permission in writing from the publisher.

For further information:
Breslov Research Institute
POB 5370, Jerusalem, Israel 91053
or:
Breslov Research Institute
POB 587, Monsey, NY 10952-0587

www.breslov.org
e-mail: info@breslov.org

Printed in Israel

"*Azamra* – I will sing"

Dedicated to my mother

Esther Egozi Garazi

…with a song in her mouth
and love in her heart…

she shows me constantly
how to find the good point in
everyone and everything

Your loving daughter,
Blanca Garazi Schoonover
Bracha *bat* **Esther**

Editor's Preface

Rebbe Nachman of Breslov repeatedly emphasized the importance of being happy: "It is a great mitzvah to be happy at all times" (*Likutey Moharan* II, 24). *Azamra!*—"I will sing!"—is his teaching about the way to happiness, by always seeking out the good points in ourselves and others.

Though simple in language, this teaching touches some of the deepest teachings of the Torah, revealed and hidden.

This book presents a translation of Rebbe Nachman's original lesson of *Azamra!* (*Likutey Moharan* I, 282), which was first given on Shemini Atzeret 5568 (October 24, 1807). The lesson is accompanied by a selection of writings in the Breslov tradition founded on the teachings of *Azamra!* Reb Noson of Breslov (1780-1844) was Rebbe Nachman's closest pupil. His Torah discourse on *Azamra!* (*Likutey Halakhot, Orach Chaim, Hilkhot Hashkamat HaBoker* 1) is presented almost in its entirety. In it, Reb Noson explores the significance of *Azamra!* in all areas of the life of the Jewish People. Also included are *chidushim*—new elaborations of Torah teachings—from the writings of later generations of Breslov leaders.

The book concludes with Reb Noson's prayer on *Azamra!* (*Likutey Tefilot* I, 90), composed in the spirit of

Rebbe Nachman's request to "turn the lessons into prayers" (*Likutey Moharan* II, 25).

In the merit of the Tzaddikim who have given us this great heritage, may we, too, fulfill these teachings until the coming of our righteous Mashiach and the rebuilding of the Holy Temple—for the Sanctuary is constructed out of the good points of every Jew. Amen.

Judging Others Favorably

"And judge all people on the scale of merit" (*Avot* 1:6).

When a person judges others favorably, he merits to eat the "fruits" of this mitzvah in this world, while the principal is reserved for him for the World to Come. Judging others favorably also promotes peace. When a person tries to interpret his friend's deeds favorably and says, "He did not wrong me in this—he acted unintentionally," or, "His intentions were good," peace reigns between them (*Rashi*).

Our Rabbis taught:

When a person judges his friend on the scale of merit, he himself is judged favorably.

The story is told of a man who came down from the Upper Galilee and hired himself out to a certain employer in the south for three years. On the day before Yom Kippur, the man said to his employer, "Give me my wages so I can go back to my wife and children."

"I have no money," the employer replied.

"Then give me fruit," the man said.

"I have none," came the reply.

"Then give me land."

"I have none."

"Then give me livestock."

"I have none."

"Then give me pillows and bedding."

"I have none."

Bitterly disappointed, the man slung his belongings onto his back and returned home, empty-handed.

A few weeks after Sukkot, the employer took the man's wages in his hand along with three donkey loads—one of food, one of drink and one of various delicacies—and traveled to the worker's house. After they had eaten and drunk, the employer gave the man his wages and asked him, "When you said to me, 'Give me my wages,' and I said, 'I have no money,' what did you suspect me of?"

"I thought that perhaps an opportunity had arisen to buy merchandise cheaply, and you had used the money for the purchase," the man replied.

"And when you said to me, 'Give me livestock,' and I said, 'I have no livestock,' what did you suspect me of?"

"I thought that perhaps your animals were hired out to others at the moment."

"And when you said to me, 'Give me land,' and I said, 'I have no land,' what did you suspect me of?"

"I thought that perhaps your land was being leased out to others."

"And when I said, 'I have no fruit,' what did you suspect me of?"

"I said, 'Perhaps his fruit has not been tithed.'"

"And when I said, 'I have no pillows and bedding,' what did you suspect me of?"

"I said, 'Perhaps he dedicated all his possessions to Heaven.'"

The employer said to him, "That is exactly what happened! I vowed away all my possessions because of Hyrkanus my son, who does not learn Torah. But when I went to my friends in the south, they absolved me from all my vows. As for you, just as you judged me favorably, the All-Present will judge you favorably."

(*Shabbat* 127b)

An outstanding classic of Jewish religious literature, *Likutey Moharan* is a collection of Rebbe Nachman's major Torah lessons and the primary source book for all his principal teachings. These lessons were given on different occasions in Rebbe Nachman's life and were written down by his pupil, Reb Noson, under the Rebbe's direct supervision. With references ranging over the entire length and breadth of the Scriptures, Talmud, Midrash, Halakhah and Kabbalah, Likutey Moharan is especially noted for its brilliant exploration of the interrelationships between words and concepts in the Hebrew language.

The teaching of *Azamra!* appears in Likutey Moharan I, 282. The first part of this lesson was originally given on Shemini Atzeret 5568 (October 24, 1807). A few days later, Rebbe Nachman left Breslov hurriedly for his mysterious journey to Lemberg. The second part of *Azamra!* was taught to Reb Noson in the carriage as the Rebbe started his journey.

Azamra!
Likutey Moharan I, 282

Azamra l'Elokai be-odee…

"I will sing to my God with the little I have left."

(Psalms 146:2)

Ve-od me'at ve-ein rasha, ve-hitbonanta al mekomo ve-einenu.

"And in but a little bit the sinner is not; you shall reflect upon his place and he will not be there."

(Psalms 37:10)

• The Good in Others…

Know! You must judge all people favorably. Even in the case of a complete sinner, you must search until you find some modicum of good by virtue of which he is *not a sinner*. By finding this small amount of good and judging him favorably, you really do elevate him to the scale of merit. You can then bring him to return to God.

This teaching is implicit in the words of the Psalm: "And in but a little bit the sinner is not; you shall reflect upon his place and he will not be there." The verse is telling us to judge everyone favorably. Even if you see that someone is a complete sinner, you must still hunt and search until you find some little bit of good in him. There, in the place where this little bit of good exists, that person is not wicked!

This is the meaning of the words of the Psalm: "And in but a *little bit* the sinner is not." In other words, you must seek out the *little bit* of good that still remains in him, for in that place he is not a sinner. Though he may be wicked, is it really possible that not even a modicum of good exists in him anymore? Could it be that he never once carried out some mitzvah or did something good in his entire life? By finding a little bit of good in him, at which point he is not a sinner, and then judging him favorably, you really do elevate him from a position of guilt to one of merit. As a result, he will return to God.

Thus, "in but a little bit the sinner is not." By finding in the sinner a little bit of good where he is not wicked, through this, "you shall reflect upon his place and he will not be there." When you reflect upon and examine his place and level, he will no longer be in his original place. For by finding in him a little bit of good, some good point, and then judging him favorably, you genuinely move him off the scale of guilt and onto the scale of merit. "You shall reflect upon his place and he will not be there." Understand this well.

...And in Ourselves

You must also find this good point within yourself. It is a known principle that one must try to be happy always and keep far away from depression.[1] It may be that when you start examining yourself, you may think you have nothing good in you at all. You see that you are full of sin, and the Evil One[2] wants to push you into depression and sadness as a result. Even so, you must not allow yourself to fall—not on any account. Instead, you should search until you find that little bit of good within yourself. For how could it be that you never did a single mitzvah or anything good in your entire life?

You may start to examine your good deed, only to see that it is also full of blemishes and devoid of purity. The very mitzvah or holy act seems to have been prompted by impure motives and bound up with improper thoughts and numerous flaws. Even so, how is it possible that this mitzvah or holy deed contains not even a modicum of good? Some good point *must* be there.

You have to search until you find some modicum of good in yourself, to restore your inner vitality and attain happiness. And by searching for and finding some little bit of good that still remains in you, you

---

1 This point is emphasized throughout Rebbe Nachman's writings. See *Advice*, Joy; *Rebbe Nachman's Wisdom* #13; *Likutey Moharan* I, 5, 22; *Likutey Moharan* II, 23, 24, etc.

2 Hebrew: ba'al davar, literally, "master of the word." This refers to the evil inclination that speaks inside each person.

elevate yourself from the scale of guilt to the scale of merit, and then you can return to God." "And in a little bit the sinner is not; you shall reflect upon his place and he will not be there."

We have seen that we have to judge *others* favorably—even the wicked—and find their good points so as to elevate them from the scale of guilt onto the scale of merit. This same teaching applies to the way a person relates to himself. You must judge yourself favorably and find the good points that still exist in you. This will give you the strength to avoid a complete fall into despair and, indeed, recover your inner vitality and bring joy to your soul with the little bit of good you find—some mitzvah or good deed you once performed.

The Melody of Life

In exactly the same way, you must carry on searching until you find yet another good point. Even if this good point is also mixed with many impurities, still, you must extract some positive point from here as well. And so you must go on—searching and gathering together additional good points. It is through this that melodies are made.

[Music, in essence, is created through the separation of good from evil—through selecting the good "wind" (Hebrew: *ruach*, which also means "spirit") and rejecting the winds of gloom and despair. To play a musical instrument—which is itself a vessel containing air—one causes the air to vibrate, producing sounds. The skill lies in moving one's hands on the instrument in such a way as to select the good vibrations—the "good wind," which makes music—and avoid the bad vibrations—the "winds of gloom and depression," which create dissonance and mere noise.[3]]

When a person refuses to let himself fall, but instead revives his spirits by searching out and finding his positive points, collecting them together and sifting them out from the impurities and evil within him—melodies are made. Then he can pray and sing and give thanks to God.

It is a known fact that when a person becomes depressed over his gross physicality and evil deeds and sees how far from holiness he really is, he becomes completely incapable of praying. He cannot even open his mouth. Depression, sadness and heaviness weigh on him when he perceives the overwhelming distance that separates him from God. But by following the path of finding the good points, he can give himself new life. Even if he knows that he has committed ruinous acts and numerous transgressions, and even if he is aware of his great distance from God, he must nevertheless

---

3 For a fuller discussion, see *Likutey Moharan* I, 54; also see *Advice*, Melody; *Rebbe Nachman's Wisdom* #273.

search through and through until he finds the good points that still exist within him. In this way, he can revitalize himself and bring himself to happiness. For it is certainly fitting that one should feel an ever-increasing joy at every good point emanating from the holy nature of his Jewishness. When a person restores his spirits and brings himself to happiness through this path, he will be able to pray, sing and give thanks to God.

"*Azamra l'Elokai be-ODee*—I will sing to my God with the little I have left." I will sing with the little I still find in myself, in accordance with the teaching of the verse, "In but a *little bit* (OD) the sinner is not." By virtue of this good point, I will be able to sing and give thanks to God. This explains the meaning of *Azamra!*—"I will sing!" I will sing the songs and melodies that are created by collecting the good points, as explained above.

[Reb Noson writes:

Our Rebbe told us emphatically to follow this teaching, for it is a major foundation for all who want to draw closer to God and not lose their eternal reward completely, God forbid.

In most cases when a person is far from God, the main reason stems from depression and sadness. He becomes depressed when he starts to look down on himself, having seen for himself the great damage he has caused through his actions. Each person knows the afflictions of his heart and his pain. As a result, he comes to look down on himself, and in most cases, despairs of himself completely. Then he doesn't pray with concentration and doesn't even practice what he is still capable of doing.

A person must use all his intelligence to fight these feelings. Whenever a person falls in his estimation of himself, it may well be true that he performed some bad actions. But the fall itself, and the consequent depression and sadness that overwhelm him, are nothing but the work of the Evil One. The Evil One tries to weaken a person's resolve with the aim of throwing him down completely. Therefore, one must be very firm and always practice this teaching of *Azamra!*—to search oneself at all times for some little good, for the good points, etc. In this way, it is possible to revive oneself and become happy again, and look forward with confidence to help from God and ultimate success. Then one will be able to pray and sing and give thanks to God—"I will sing to my God with the little I have left"—and return to God with true sincerity, just as the Rebbe explains.]

• The Prayer Leader

And know: The one who is capable of creating these melodies—namely, collecting the good points that can be found in every Jew, even sinners—can lead the communal prayers. For the prayer leader is called the *shaliach tzibur*, the messenger of the people, and he must be sent by all the people. His job is to gather every good point to be found in every single one of the worshippers. All these good points must be merged within him. When he stands in prayer, he does so with all this good. This is the idea of the "messenger of the people." The one who fulfills this role must have within him this exalted aspect of being able to gather together the good points, so that all these points will be drawn to him, merging within him.

The one who can compose these melodies by judging all people favorably—even the wicked and those of little worth—through constantly searching and seeking to find good points in all of them, whereby melodies are composed…the Tzaddik who attains this level can be the *chazzan* and the people's messenger, leader of the communal prayers. For he has what is needed to be a truly fitting messenger of the people in that all the good points are drawn to him and merged within him. He is capable of gathering all the good points that are to be found in each and every Jew, even sinners.

• A Holy Sanctuary

And know: In every generation, there is a shepherd, a Moses—for Moses was "the faithful shepherd"—and this shepherd makes a sanctuary. And know: Little schoolchildren receive the undefiled breath of their mouths from this sanctuary.

When a child begins to read and enters the study of Torah, he is first taught the verse, "And He called to Moses" (*Leviticus* 1:1; see *Vayikra Rabbah* 7:3).[4] The Book of Leviticus begins right after the Sanctuary in the desert was erected. God calls to Moses and begins speaking with him from the Sanctuary: "And He called to Moses." Small children begin studying Torah from this point because it is from here that they receive the breath of their mouths. Here they start to read and enter into the study of Torah.

And know: All the Tzaddikim of the generation, each and every one of them, play the role of this shepherd. For each one of them is a Moses, and each, in his own way, makes a sanctuary—the sanctuary from which schoolchildren receive the breath of their mouths. Likewise, each Tzaddik, in accordance with his nature and the nature of the sanctuary that he constructs, has children who receive from there. Consequently, each and every Tzaddik of the generation has a certain

---

4 In a Torah scroll, the word *Vayikra*, "And He called," is written with an *aleph ze'irah*, a small aleph. This Aramaic term literally means "teach the small"—i.e., the children. For a fuller discussion of the significance of the small aleph in relation to the lesson of *Azamra!*, see *Likutey Halakhot, Eruvey Techumin* 6.

number of children who receive the breath of their mouths from him—each child in accordance with his nature.

The Sages expressed this idea when they said, "The children are snatched away because of the sin of the generation, as it is written, 'And pasture your kids by the shepherds' tents (*MiSHKaNot*).' The children are taken instead (*shemitMaSHKNin*) of the shepherds" (Shabbat 33b).

"By the shepherds' tents" alludes to where children receive the breath of their mouths—from the "tents," or sanctuaries, of the "shepherds"—the Tzaddikim of the generation, each of whom makes a sanctuary, as mentioned above.

The one who can comprehend all this—that is, know which children relate to each Tzaddik and how much they receive from him, and understand all the concepts involved in this and the generations that will come from them to the very end—is the one who can compose the melodies mentioned above.

This reveals the hidden meaning of what our Sages said in the Mishnah, "In truth, they said, the schoolmaster sees where the children are reading" (Shabbat 11a). The schoolmaster (Hebrew: *chazzan*, which can also mean "cantor" and "seer")—namely, the one who can compose the melodies mentioned above—*he* can be the *chazzan*, the people's messenger, leader of the communal prayers. He sees and knows "where the children are reading." That is, he knows from which Tzaddik they receive the breath of their mouths in order to read and enter into the study of Torah.

[Reb Noson adds:

Understand these words well. It is impossible to explain everything. Each person's life is unique, but this teaching is universal; it applies at all times in life, in youth and old age. The lesson of *Azamra!* can always revive us. Happy are those who take it to heart.]

The Beginning of My Journey

No details survive about the occasion on which the first part of *Azamra!* was revealed, on Shemini Atzeret 5568 (October 24, 1807). By that time, Rebbe Nachman was already suffering from the tuberculosis that would claim his life three years hence. Two days later, on the day after *Isru Chag*, Rebbe Nachman set off hurriedly from Breslov for a journey to Lemberg. He never revealed the exact purpose of this trip; like all his journeys, it was shrouded in great mystery. But as he sat in the carriage on the first stage of his trip, he said to Reb Noson, "I will tell you the beginning of my journey." He proceeded to reveal the second part of *Azamra!*

Reb Noson writes:

"The Rebbe was in a great hurry to start traveling. As for us, our hearts still burned to follow after him and feast our eyes on his holy face and hear more from his holy lips. His carriage was already moving off at a rapid pace. I started running after the carriage, even though it is very hard to keep up on foot with a carriage drawn by strong horses. But the carriage reached a hill and had to slow down. I caught up and once again came before the splendor of his holiness. My friend Rabbi Naftali had seen me running after the carriage and had come running after me. ...

"We stood there in front of the Rebbe and he gave us a kindly look. 'Which would you prefer,' he asked, 'that I give you a blessing or teach you Torah?' 'Give us the blessing when you return home in peace from Lemberg,' I answered. 'Now teach us Torah!' I knew that if we did not hear it at once, it would be lost forever. He said, 'I will tell you the beginning of my journey'—and it was then that he revealed the secret of how each of the Tzaddikim builds a sanctuary. When the Rebbe had concluded, the three of us took our leave and kissed him on the hand. The Rebbe then went on his way to Lemberg. I carried on running after him as long as I could still see the carriage. Eventually it disappeared from sight, and then I returned."

(*Yemey Moharnat* 23a)

Lemberg (now known as Lvov) was the capital of Galicia. Since the first partition of Poland in 1772, Lemberg had been in Austrian hands. The Jews living under Austrian rule were being urged to abandon their traditional way of life and adopt gentile culture. Traditionally, Lemberg was one of the foremost centers of Torah learning in Eastern Europe. It would soon emerge as one of the first centers of the *Haskalah*, the Enlightenment movement, which changed the face of European Jewry. At the time of Rebbe Nachman's visit, a circle of Jewish intellectuals espousing the new culture resided in Lemberg, and Rebbe Nachman had contact with them. The Rebbe also underwent medical treatment for his tuberculosis.

Rabbi Nachman of Tcherin writes:

"The Rebbe saw with his holy spirit that atheism and skepticism were destined to rise up against the Jewish People. In Lemberg, he worked to subjugate those trends. In most cases when a person first entertains such ideas, it is the result of the sense of discouragement he feels when he starts thinking about all his sins. It is hard for him to remain firm or encourage himself with one of the good points that still remain in him. The end result is that he falls completely and gets into ways that are totally bad. He loses his faith completely and becomes an atheist.

"When the Rebbe returned from Lemberg, he decried the atheism that was spreading more and more throughout the world. Today we can actually see how everything he said has come about. The cancer of atheism and unbelief has grown widespread. The main thrust of the attack focuses on the young. They are brought up from their earliest years to be skeptical about the teachings of the Rabbis and Sages. This is very common all over. The Rebbe labored to rectify this situation. This was the purpose of his journey to Lemberg, and this was why he said, 'I will tell you the beginning of my journey.'"

(*Parparaot LeChokhmah* 282)

At Rebbe Nachman's request, Reb Noson used the ideas in Likutey Moharan and the Rebbe's other teachings to illuminate the practical meaning of the laws in the Shulchan Arukh—the standard legal compendium governing all aspects of Jewish life.[5] The eight volumes of Likutey Halakhot follow the exact order of the subject headings of the Shulchan Arukh, with one or more discourses on each subject. They cover themes drawn from the Torah, Talmud, Midrash, Zohar and Kabbalah, while at the same time serving as the basic commentary on Likutey Moharan itself. The first discourse in Likutey Halakhot, Orach Chaim, Hilkhot Hashkamat HaBoker 1, is founded on the teaching of Azamra! and demonstrates the relevance of this lesson in all areas of Jewish life.

---

5 The *Shulchan Arukh* was compiled in the sixteenth century by Rabbi Josef Karo, the *Bet Yosef* (1488-1575), with glosses added by Rabbi Moses Isserles (1530-1573), the *Rema*.

Likutey Halakhot
Orach Chaim, Hilkhot Hashkamat HaBoker 1

"One should strengthen himself like a lion to rise up in the early morning in the service of his Creator, awakening the dawn."

(*Bet Yosef*)

"I shall place the Lord before me always: this is a most important principle in the Torah."

(*Rema*)

• Waking Up

When a person feels distant from God, believing that his sins and spiritual deficiencies have separated him from any good, this is a state of "sleep," which is one-sixtieth of death itself (*Berakhot* 57b). But when he begins to seek out his positive points and takes heart from the fragments of good still left in him, the joy and arousal he experiences in his devotion to God are themselves a "waking up" from sleep.

"God, how numerous my enemies have become; many are those who rise against me. There are many who say about my soul, 'There is no help for him in the Lord.'…I lay down and slept, but I awoke, for God sustains me. I will not fear the tens of thousands of people who have set themselves round about, against me."

(Psalms 3:2-3, 6-7)

The "enemies" of whom King David speaks are the enemies of the soul—namely, a person's sins and spiritual blemishes. They attack by making it seem as if there is no hope left for a person, attempting to throw him down completely: "There are many who say of my soul: 'There is no help for him in the Lord.'" Such an assault of negative thoughts puts a person into a state of "sleep": "I lay down and slept." The truth, however, is that it is forbidden to despair. One must fight back and wake up from his sleep by finding the little bit of good still left within him. Thus the Psalm continues: "I *awoke*, for God sustains me."

"For God sustains me"—in what sense? The good point that a person finds in himself is a part of Godliness, for all good emanates from God. The Torah, the Jewish People and the Holy One are a unity (*Zohar*, Introduction). Accordingly, when a good point exists in a Jew—be it a mitzvah or a good deed—this good is completely bound in unity with God. For, "God is good to all" (Psalms 145:9), and, "Taste and see that God is good" (Psalms 34:9). Any good that exists, in whatever form, emanates from God. This is the sense in which "God sustains me." The good point that a person finds within himself—that modicum of Godliness—sustains him and arouses him from his slumber.

Confident in the awareness of this good point, a

person can declare: "I shall not fear the tens of thousands of people who have set themselves round about, against me." Even if there seem to be tens of thousands of sins and blemishes rising up against him and seeking to throw him down, he is no longer afraid. Having found some good point remaining, he awakens from his sleep and raises himself onto the scale of merit, which brings him to return to God. The little bit of good he finds to lift himself up casts aside all the evil—because a little light can chase away much darkness (*Tzaydah LaDerekh* 12).

"I have awoken; I am still (*ve-ODee*) with You."

(Psalms 139:18)

By virtue of the "little bit" that he still (*OD*) finds—the good point that is bound up with Godliness and is therefore "still with You"—by virtue of this, "I have awoken."

Darkness and Light

"Awake my glory, awake the lyre and the harp; I will awaken the dawn."

(Psalms 57:9)

To find the good points within oneself corresponds to "awakening the dawn"—because the good point is itself "dawn." Dawn is the moment at which light appears out of the darkness. Interestingly, the Hebrew word for dawn, *ShaChaR*, has the same letters as the word for darkness, *ShaChoR*.

The idea of the good point is also present in the words, "I am black (*SheChoRah*) but comely, daughters of Jerusalem" (Song of Songs 1:5). A person's good point seems to be blackened and tarnished by his many sins and blemishes; it lies buried beneath his own darkness and gloom. When he judges himself favorably and uncovers it, his good point responds: "I am black but comely...do not look down upon me because I am black" (ibid., 1:6). Meaning: "The blackness is not my own, for 'I have been scorched by the sun'" (see *Rashi*, ad loc.). Intrinsically, the good point that exists in every person—even sinners—is very comely and beautiful. It is just that blackness has covered it over—until it is awakened.

Our Sages have taught, "'I am black'—because of the Golden Calf, 'but comely'—because of the building of the Sanctuary" (*Shir HaShirim Rabbah* 1:5). The sin of the Golden Calf encompasses all the sins in the world, for "when a person worships an idol, it is as if he denies the entire Torah" (*Chulin* 5a). Immediately after the sin of the Golden Calf, the Jewish People were commanded to build the Sanctuary. God reconciled with them as a result of Moses' devoted self-sacrifice and prayer on their behalf. Moses was able to find a positive point in even the most unworthy individual (*Likutey Moharan* I, 282; II, 82). Therefore he could pray for them at all times, even after they had transgressed the entire Torah through the sin of the Golden Calf. Even then he could find their good points, which is why he asked: "Why, God, does Your anger burn against Your people?" (Exodus 32:11). By finding the good in them, Moses completely chased away the evil. Their sins no longer held any significance because of the good that they still possessed. Accordingly, there was no longer any cause for anger.

After this episode, God taught Moses the order of prayer and revealed to him the Thirteen Attributes of Divine Mercy. "And He said, I will make all My good pass before you" (Exodus 33:19). God revealed all His good to Moses in order to teach him that God is constantly good to all. Thus it is possible to arouse the good even in the very worst person, elevating him to the scale of merit and bringing him back to God.

Knowing this, we can begin to understand the Thirteen Attributes of Divine Mercy (based on the ARI):

God, God, (1) omnipotent Lord, (2) merciful and (3) kind, (4,5) slow to anger with (6) abundant love and (7) truth. He remembers (8) lovingkindness for (9) thousands, forgiving (10) sin, (11) rebellion and (12) error, and He (13) cleanses (Exodus 34:6-7).

Full of mercy and good to all, God delays His anger and shows patience to the righteous and wicked alike. He acts this way because He inclines towards the attribute of love and judges all favorably. He finds good points even in sinners, and so tilts the scale to the side of merit.

"He remembers lovingkindness for thousands": This means that the lovingkindness of God, through which He judges all favorably and finds the positive point in everyone, is remembered and invoked in sweetening the judgments *for thousands*. Even if a man has committed thousands and myriads of blemishes, the little bit of good that God finds in him through His lovingkindness pushes everything away. Having removed the blemishes, God forgives "sin, rebellion and error" because the sinner has genuinely moved onto the scale of merit.

The Building of the Sanctuary

Moses was entirely good, as the Torah relates, "And she saw him that he was *good*" (Exodus 2:2). Consequently, Moses was always able to find the good in everyone, even in sinners. Through him, God was reconciled with the Jewish People, and commanded them to build the Sanctuary. Each person contributed to the building of the Sanctuary in accordance with the prompting of his heart. The good within each Jew had been aroused, and each one, in accordance with his individual good, brought his donation.

The Sanctuary itself was constructed out of all the good that had been sifted out from each and every Jew. Thus the Torah tells us that the people were told to bring "gold, silver and copper; sky-blue, purple and scarlet wool" (Exodus 25:3-4). These are the Supernal Colors, which correspond to the good that exists in every Jew and which are hinted at in God's words to the Jewish People, "Israel, in whom I will take pride (*etPa'ER*)" (Isaiah 49:3). The Hebrew root *Pe'ER* connotes the beauty of color. The Jewish People encompass the Supernal Colors in their brilliance—i.e., the good points that exist in every Jew, even the least of them, for each has his own unique good point which is not found in any other (cf. *Likutey Moharan* I, 34). For this, God takes pride in them. The Sanctuary contained all these colors, donated as they were by each Jew in accordance with the generosity of his heart. Thus the Sanctuary was constructed out of the good points of the Jews.

After the sin of the Golden Calf, Moses was obliged to search out the good points in each Jew. Thereafter, the Jews were commanded to construct the Sanctuary, built as it was from their good points. "'I am black'—because of the Golden Calf, 'but comely'—because of the building of the Sanctuary."

The idea that the Sanctuary was constructed out of all the good found in every Jew is implicit in *Azamra!* This concept underlies Rebbe Nachman's statement that the one who can find all the good that exists in the Jewish People—the *chazzan* or prayer leader—is the same one who can understand all the concepts involved in the sanctuary constructed by each Tzaddik of the generation. The relation between the thoughts in *Azamra!* should now be clear.

• Morning: A Time of Love

We have seen that in order to wake up, we must "awaken the dawn" (Psalms 57:9). We must arouse the good point in ourselves, which is called "dawn" (*ShaChaR*). "I am black (*SheChoRah*) but comely" (Song of Songs 1:5). When we use this means to rise up from our sleep—our spiritual fall—we also "awake the lyre and the harp." Through finding the good points, melodies are made, as explained in Rebbe Nachman's lesson.

All these ideas are implicit in the words of the *Shulchan Arukh*. "One should strengthen himself like a lion to rise up in the early morning in the service of his Creator": This tells us that a person must force himself to wake up from his sleep, his spiritual fall. How? By "awakening the dawn"—by arousing his good points, which, as we have seen, embody the concept of "dawn."

Morning, the time for this awakening, corresponds to the influence of Abraham, the man of lovingkindness (cf. *Zohar* I, 203). By inclining towards the quality of lovingkindness and judging oneself on the scale of merit, a person can rouse himself from his "sleep." Abraham used his leaning towards lovingkindness to find good in everyone, thereby making converts and drawing the world closer to God.

The words of the *Bet Yosef* are immediately followed by the gloss of the *Rema*, who cites the words of the Psalm, "I have placed God before me always." What is the connection? It means: I am forever placing and setting God before my eyes. Though I am distant from Him, He is "before me always" in the sense that I always find a good point in myself.

This same verse contains the teaching of *Azamra!*: "I shall place God before me always; He is at my right hand, I will not be moved" (Psalms 16:8). "I shall place God before me always": even if I descend to the lowest levels, God forbid. "I will not be moved": because "He is at my right hand." The "right hand" alludes to the Kabbalistic concept of the right side, embodied in the figure of Abraham and identified with the quality of lovingkindness. Through this lovingkindness, which implies judging favorably, "I will not be moved."

The Daily Prayers

Night is the time of sleep. According to the Kabbalah, at night the Shekhinah extracts the sparks of holiness that have fallen under the control of the Other Side. Correspondingly, a person who finds himself overcome by "sleep" must search for the good points, enabling himself to wake up.

Therefore King David said: "I will recall my melody in the night. I meditate with my heart and my spirit (*ruach*) searches" (Psalms 77:7). One hunts and searches for the good wind (*ruach*), the good point. Through this, melodies are created. By strengthening ourselves to find the good point and wake up from our sleep, we attain true prayer. Discovering one's good points is the foundation of prayer, as explained in *Azamra!:* "I will *sing* to my God." How? *"Be-odee*—with the little I have left"—namely, the good point.

This teaching unfolds in the order of the Morning Service. We begin our prayers by reciting the chapters describing the sacrifices and incense-offering in the Temple. The sacrifices and incense-offering exemplify the process of separating and selecting, elevating good points from the animal domain and from levels of utmost physicality. In particular, the sacrifices achieve an elevation from the level of animal to the level of man.

The incense-offering demonstrates how good can be found, even in sinners. Among the ingredients that make up the incense is galbanum, a foul-smelling substance. From the fact that the incense is incomplete without this ingredient, the Sages learned, "Any communal prayer that does not include the prayer of the sinner is no prayer" (*Keritot* 6b). Just as the burning of the incense releases the sparks of goodness, prayer is founded upon the finding of good points even in sinners (who resemble galbanum). Altogether, eleven ingredients comprised the incense—galbanum and another ten ingredients. These ten ingredients correspond to the Ten Types of Melody[6] that are created through finding the good points, even in sinners.

Speech

"O My dove trapped in the clefts of the rock, in the concealment of the cliff. Show Me your countenance; let Me hear your voice. For your voice is sweet and your countenance comely."

(Song of Songs 2:14)

When we recite the passages describing the sacrifices, it is as if we are offering the sacrifices themselves. As our Sages say, "When one studies the laws of the burnt-offering, it is considered as if he actually brought

---

6 See *Rebbe Nachman's Tikkun* (Breslov Research Institute).

a burnt-offering" (*Berakhot* 26b). Saying the words is tantamount to bringing the offering because the main intent of the sacrifices lies in the realm of *speech*. The sacrifices serve to elevate the sparks of goodness in the inanimate, vegetable and animal realms to the realm of man, whose uniqueness centers on the faculty of speech.

When the good points rise up from the lowest of levels, they must be elevated to the level of speech. At first, before the good is visible and separated out from the bad that covers it over, it is "dumb"—without the faculty of speech—as it is written, "I was struck dumb, muted; I had no comfort" (Psalms 39:3). When the good is revealed, the essential revelation and elevation that result give birth to the faculty of speech.

"O My dove trapped in the clefts of the rock, in the concealment of the cliff": The good point in a person is referred to as the "dove"—for the dove is faithful to her mate and never abandons him (cf. *Shir HaShirim Rabbah* 4). The good point that exists in each individual, even the lowliest, is always attached to God, no matter where it may be. When it falls into the depths of the repressive forces[7] that surround it on all sides, God says to it, "Show Me your countenance; let Me hear your voice.

---

7 Hebrew: *kelipot*.

For your voice is sweet and your countenance comely." Even though you are trapped in the concealment of the cliff on the lowest level, you yourself are most comely—"I am black but comely." Reveal yourself, God says, and show Me your countenance, for your good point is always comely. Find and reveal the beauty of your good point, and through this, "Let Me hear your voice." Through revealing the good point, we can *speak* (i.e., give thanks and praise to God), whereas before we could not speak at all.

"You who dwell in the gardens, companions hearken to your voice—let Me hear it."
(Song of Songs 8:13)

According to *Rashi*, "dwelling in the gardens" implies the state of exile amongst the nations. This alludes to the good points dwelling amongst the evil desires and shortcomings embodied by the various peoples of the world (see *Likutey Moharan* I, 36). God yearns for the good points to burst into speech: "Companions hearken to your voice—let Me hear it." God desires that the good points be revealed and their voices heard in song and praise to Him.

The sacrificial offerings parallel the process of elevating the good points so that they will be revealed and expressed in speech. This explains why one who studies the passages dealing with the sacrifices, using his faculty of speech, is credited for offering those sacrifices. For the goal of the sacrifices lies in the realm of speech.

The Sanctuary and the Work of Creation

Every day in the Temple, when priests offered the sacrifices and the Levites stood on their platform chanting, a deputation of Israelites stood by and recited the account of the Creation (Genesis 1) and the Song of Moses (*Ha'azinu*, Deuteronomy 32; cf. *Ta'anit* 26a).

Since the main intent of the sacrifices is to find and separate out the good point from the midst of the animal impurities, it is specifically the priest who conducts these rites. The priest is "the man of lovingkindness," as exemplified in the person of Abraham, about whom it is written, "You shall be a priest forever" (Psalms 110:4). By inclining towards the quality of lovingkindness and judging all favorably, one can find the good points even on the lowest of levels. This is the intent of the sacrifices.

In the same way, melodies are made. Therefore the Levites stood on their platform, chanting and playing music—for through the revelation of good accomplished by the priest, the man of lovingkindness, melodies are created. And the deputation of Israelites that stood by, engaged in Torah study, represents the faculty of speech—because the intent of the sacrifices is to raise good to its consummate level, the level of speech.

To understand why the Israelite deputation first recited the account of Creation, we must understand that the essence of the Act of Creation lay in the separating out of good. Thus we say, "In His goodness He renews each day, continually, the Act of Creation" (Morning Liturgy), and regarding each of the six days of Creation, it is written, "it was good" (Genesis 1). Prior to the rectification brought about by the Act of Creation, the Torah states, "The earth was formless and void, with darkness upon the face of the deep" (Genesis 1:2). This reflects the concept of the prevailing evil covering over the good. The rectification came about through "the spirit of God hovering on the waters" (ibid.). This is the spirit of Mashiach, the very essence of goodness; indeed, all the good points found in each Jew are "sparks of Mashiach."

The world is basically sustained and built through the "spirit of God," the good spirit, the spirit of Mashiach. Through this spirit, good points can be found even in the midst of the formlessness and void, and through this, God can say, "'Let there be light.' And there was light" (ibid., 1:3). Then God can divide "between the light and the darkness" (ibid., 1:4). Having found the good point in himself, a person can genuinely move onto the scale of merit, and then the light is revealed and the darkness is separated from the light, the evil from the good, and so on. Thus the very essence of the Act of Creation involves the finding and separating out of the good point.

We are taught that "the form of the Sanctuary was patterned after the form of Creation" (*Tikkuney Zohar*, Introduction). The Sanctuary, too, was constructed from the good that is separated out from evil. The deputation of Israelites that stood by as the sacrifices were offered recited the account of Creation since the sacrifices were an aspect of the work of Creation—the separating out of good from evil. By the same token, the place for the sacrificial offerings lay in the Sanctuary, and later, the Temple—for the Sanctuary and Temple are also constructed through the separating out of good. Thus the place of the Temple is called "this *good* mountain" (Deuteronomy 3:25).

The Israelite deputation also recited the Song of Moses, in which Moses promised that the Torah would never be forgotten (cf. Deuteronomy 31:21: "This Song will testify for them like a witness"). Even in the ultimate concealment, when "I will utterly hide My face" (ibid., 31:18), this Song serves as a witness. The Song conveys that even if the Jewish People are far from God—even in the ultimate concealment—nevertheless, they are still close to Him, because there are still good points in them, even in the very lowliest. The Song proclaims, "But His nation remained God's portion; Jacob is the lot of His heritage. He found them in a desolate land" (ibid., 32:9-10). Even in a desolate and formless land, "His nation remained God's portion," for the good points that remain within a person constitute his portion of Godliness. The Israelite deputation recited this Song as the sacrifices were offered because songs and melodies are made through the discovery of the good points, even in a "desolate land."

• *Pesukey D'zimra*—Song

Following the recitation of the chapters dealing with the sacrifices and incense-offering comes the next section of the Morning Service, *Pesukey D'zimra*, Verses of Song. First the sacrifices bring about the separation of the good points from even the lowest levels, and then, from finding the good points, melodies—the Psalms—are made. The actual verse upon which the teaching of *Azamra!* is based—"I will sing to my God with the little I have left" (Psalms 146:2)—is part of *Pesukey D'zimra*.

• **Building the House of Prayer**

After the *Pesukey D'zimra*, the Morning Service continues with the recitation of the Shema and the blessings that accompany it. In the first blessing,

Yotzer Or, we bless God for renewing the work of Creation, which "He renews in His goodness each day, continually" (Morning Liturgy). As we have seen, Creation and the Sanctuary are one concept, for "the form of the Sanctuary was patterned after the form of Creation" (*Tikkuney Zohar,* Introduction, p. 13a). The blessing of *Yotzer Or* thus corresponds to the building of the Sanctuary, which was constructed out of the good points of the Jewish People. In the Sanctuary, prayer achieves its perfection.

"For My house shall be called a house of prayer for all the nations, says the Lord God, Who gathers in the outcasts of Israel."

(Isaiah 56:7-8)

The building of the Temple, the House of God, comes about through God's gathering in the outcasts of Israel. God does this by finding the good points even in the outcasts and those without hope, and gathers them in to the side of holiness. Similarly, the Holy Temple of the future—"this good mountain" (Deuteronomy 3:25)—will be constructed through the good which the righteous redeemer, the Mashiach, will gather together. Because the discovery of the good points forms the foundation of prayer, prayer achieves its perfection in the Sanctuary, built as it is out of the good points.

Now we can understand why the *Amidah*, the Standing Prayer, the climax of the Morning Service, is preceded by the recitation of the chapters dealing with the sacrifices, then the *Pesukey D'zimra*, and then by the Shema and its blessings. Through the passages dealing with the sacrifices, the good points are separated out. From them, melodies and songs (the *Pesukey D'zimra*) are made. Then we can build the Sanctuary, the place of prayer (the blessings accompanying the Shema, which include our blessing of God for "renewing the work of Creation each day, continually," and which acknowledge that "the form of the Sanctuary was patterned after the form of Creation"). From this Sanctuary, "little children receive the undefiled breath of their mouths." This correlates to the words of the Shema itself: "And you shall teach them diligently *to your children*" (ibid., 6:7), and, "you shall teach them *to your children*, speaking of them" (ibid., 11:19).

The unification of God's Name through the Shema comes about through the good points that are separated out from evil. Through this process of separation, the Holy One is united with the Shekhinah. By finding the good points—even in sinners—holiness is elevated from the very depths of the Other Side. The Shekhinah prides herself on these good points, as if to say, "See with what a child I come to You!" With the discovery of each good point, she prides herself more and more, because God's glory is exalted precisely when that which was furthest from Him draws near.[8] Thus the *Zohar* teaches: "When Jethro, who had pursued every possible type of idolatry, came to join the Jewish People, the Name of God was truly glorified above and below" (*Zohar* II, 71). Precisely when the good points that were sunken in the greatest depths are raised up and elevated, the Shekhinah takes the greatest pride, as it were. Through this, the unification of the Holy One and the Shekhinah takes place: "Hear O Israel, the Lord our God, the Lord is One."

"The Sanctuary was then one (whole)" (Exodus 26:6). All the good points are now merged in the unity of God, whereupon we begin the *Amidah*. We start with the words, "My God, open my lips and my mouth shall declare Your praise" (Psalms 51:17). Through all the stages in the service leading up to this point, we have found the good points, made from them a Sanctuary, and united the Holy One with the Shekhinah. Now we can open our mouths to *speak*. The ultimate ascent of good is its elevation to the level of speech. This is what we ask for now: "My God, open my lips and my mouth shall declare Your praise."

---

[8] This point is discussed in a number of places in Rebbe Nachman's writings; see especially *Likutey Moharan* I, 14.

• Clothes

The first thing we do in the morning is get dressed. One should begin by holding his garment on the right-hand side (see *Shulchan Arukh, Orach Chaim* 2:4), in accordance with the principle that one should always endeavor to strengthen and give priority to the right side as opposed to the left.

To understand the significance of this teaching, we must recall that the right side is the side of loving-kindness—the quality through which we find the good points in ourselves. By finding the good points, we not only rouse ourselves from "sleep" (as discussed above), but we also make garments to clothe the soul. So long as the good was not yet revealed—namely, during the time of "sleep"—the soul was naked.

Among the Morning Blessings (recited at the very beginning of the Morning Service, immediately after rising) is the blessing, "Who clothes the naked." Through the revelation of good points, garments are made—the garments of the soul. God adorns Himself, as it were, with the good points of the Jewish People, as it is written, "Israel, in whom I will take pride (*etPaER*)" (Isaiah 49:3); through these good points, garments of beauty (*Pe'ER*) and honor are made. These refer to the tzitzit and tefilin, the "clothing" of the soul. The *Zohar* (*Bereshit* 23) explains that the verse, "For that is his only covering; it is the robe for his skin" (Exodus 22:26) refers to the tzitzit and tefilin. The tzitzit and tefilin are made from the good points that are separated out at night. It follows that man's "garments"—his clothes of beauty, encompassing all the colors—are made of the good points, for the good points encompass all the colors, as we saw earlier. This explains why, when dressing, it is necessary to "strengthen the right side." Our "clothes" are made up of the good points—which we find by inclining towards the right side, towards the quality of lovingkindness.

• The Morning Blessings

The idea of praising God for helping us find the good points so we can wake up from our sleep and our spiritual fall characterizes all the Morning Blessings.

The first blessing speaks of how God "gives understanding to the heart to distinguish between day and night." The good point is "day" and the evil which covers it over is "night" and "darkness." In the process of finding the good point, evil is separated from it, distinguishing between "day" and "night."

The second blessing speaks of how God "did not make me a heathen." Were a person unable to find the good point in himself, he would be in danger of falling completely, to the point that he would, in effect, become a heathen. Accordingly, now that he has roused and strengthened himself with God's help to find his good point, he gives thanks and praise to God because He "did not make me a heathen."

Later come the three blessings, "He opens the eyes of the blind," "He loosens those who were bound," and, "He straightens those who were bent down." When a person is in a state of "sleep" and spiritual descent, he resembles a blind person groping in the darkness. It is as if he were imprisoned and bent down. He is able to find his good point only because God opens his eyes. Then he is released from his imprisonment and raised upright instead of being stooped over. By finding the good point, he elevates himself from the scale of guilt onto the scale of merit, and is able to return to God.

All the other Morning Blessings refer to this theme. The last blessing is, "Who gives strength to the weary." Even when one is overwhelmed with weariness, he can still wake up from his sleep with the strength God gives him. Hence this final blessing speaks of how God "causes sleep to pass from my eyes," and concludes by thanking God for "bestowing lovingkindnesses." Through lovingkindness, the good points are revealed.

• Phases of the Moon

According to the Midrash, God created the moon and the sun of equal size. However, the moon was jealous of the sun and complained that the heaven and earth could not have two luminaries of equal size. Because the moon intruded unlawfully into the sphere of the sun (the moon is sometimes visible by day), God diminished its size. Then God appeased the moon by surrounding it with stars, like a viceroy encircled by his assistants. (*Bereshit Rabbah* 6:3,4; *Pirkei d'Rabbi Eliezer* 6).

"And the enlightened will shine like the brightness of the firmament, and those who turn the many to righteousness will be like the stars forever."

(Daniel 12:3)

[At the beginning of each month, the slender crescent of the new moon becomes visible. The moon steadily waxes until it reaches the full-moon phase at the midpoint of the month. Then it begins to wane, diminishing to the point that it becomes invisible at the end of the month. Prior to the fixing of the Jewish calendar by Hillel II in 4119 (358-9 C.E.), a new month was deemed to have begun only after the *Bet Din* "sanctified" it, based on the testimony of two reliable witnesses who had seen the new moon itself (*Rosh HaShanah* 24a). Today we give thanks for the appearance of the new moon in the ceremony of *kiddush levanah*, sanctification of the moon, which is recited upon seeing the moon clearly in the nighttime sky between the third day of its appearance and the fifteenth of the month (*Shulchan Arukh, Orach Chaim* 426:1-3). The Sages say, "Whoever pronounces the benediction of the new moon in its due time welcomes, as it were, the presence of the Shekhinah" (*Sanhedrin* 42a; *Sofrim* 20,1).]

Periods when the Jewish People are on a spiritually low level can be seen as times of the "incomplete moon," a time when the moon stands accused. The incomplete moon is the source of all sins and blemishes (*Chulin* 60b). But when a Jew arouses himself and finds his good points, thereby returning to God, this corresponds to the "restoration of the moon" from its blemish. Then the "sanctification of the moon" can take place.

At the beginning of the month, when we look for the moon in order to sanctify it, the moon appears very small and fine—a mere point. This is the good point, which is "black but comely." When the moon reaches its ultimate diminution at the end of the month, it is necessary for the entire Jewish People to search for it, until two witnesses can testify to having seen a small point of the new moon. Then the *Bet Din* proclaims the new month and the moon is "restored." This process parallels the manner in which the good point that we succeed in finding in ourselves, no matter how infinitesimally small it may be, raises us from the scale of guilt onto the scale of merit.

After receiving testimony from the witnesses who spotted the moon, the *Bet Din* and all the people would proclaim: "Sanctified, sanctified" (*Rosh HaShanah* 24a). Similarly, when we find even a small good point, we become sanctified by judging ourselves and others favorably. The moon was diminished in size because of its complaint. *Words*—namely, the proclamation, "Sanctified, sanctified"—elevate the moon from its blemish. The sanctification of the moon depends on the single point of light that was seen.

After God diminished the size of the moon, He gave it the stars as a consolation. The stars allude to the good points found in all Jews, through which they can move onto the scale of merit by being judged favorably. It is written, "Those who turn the many to righteousness will be like the stars forever" (Daniel 12:3). Those who turn the many to righteousness are the Tzaddikim of each generation, who judge all favorably. Because of this, even the sinners move onto the scale of merit. "Like the stars forever": because the stars are the good points. Later in the same passage, it is written: "Many will be purified, whitened and refined, while the wicked will do wickedly and not understand" (ibid., 12:10). Then the "enlightened will shine…and those who turn the many to righteousness will be like the stars forever." This refers to the era of the Mashiach, the end of days, when the forces of evil will attack most powerfully, as we find in the statements of our Sages. At that time, a great process of selection and refinement will take place. "Many will be purified, whitened and refined": The main rectification will be brought about by turning the many to righteousness. The most important spiritual work of the Tzaddikim will be to judge everyone favorably, finding the good points of even the very lowly. Through this process, the final redemption will take place with the coming of Mashiach.

King David says, "Praise Him, all you stars of light" (Psalms 148:3). Through the light-giving stars—the good points—we are able to give thanks and praise to God. "I will sing to my God with the little I have left." Thus the moon was given the stars as a consolation. The stars—the good points—serve to rectify the blemishes of the moon.

• *Tikkun Chatzot*—The Midnight Lament

A person who wishes to rise early to plead before his Creator should aspire to pray at the times when the night watches change…for at those hours, one's prayers over the destruction of the Temple and the exile are especially accepted (*Shulchan Arukh, Orach Chaim* 1:3). This teaching refers to *Tikkun Chatzot*, the Midnight Lament, which is found in complete editions of the prayer book. The time for *Tikkun Chatzot* is the middle of the night, regardless of whether the nights are short or long.

(*Mishnah Berurah on Orach Chaim* 1:3)

Did King David know the exact time of midnight? Even our teacher Moses did not know it. For it is written, "About midnight I will go out into the midst of Egypt" (Exodus 11:4). Why "about midnight"? Can there be any doubt in the mind of Heaven? We must therefore say that God told Moses, "At midnight," and Moses came and said, "About midnight." Hence Moses was in doubt. Can David have known it, then? David had a sign. ...A harp hung above David's bed. As soon as midnight arrived, a north wind came and blew upon it, and [the harp] played by itself. [David] arose immediately and began studying Torah until daybreak.

(*Berakhot* 3b)

To rise up at midnight for *Tikkun Chatzot*, we must break the heaviness of sleep. We do this by finding the good points, as we saw earlier in connection with the verse, "Awake my glory, awake the lyre and the harp" (Psalms 57:9; see above, p. 34). The "harp" is King David's harp, which was played by the north wind— the "good wind" or "good spirit"—namely, the good point. The Hebrew word for north, *TZaFoN*, carries the connotations of "hidden" and "concealed." The good point is concealed in the depths of sleep. Yet it exists, even in the least worthy of people. "How great is Your goodness (i.e. the good point) which You have kept hidden (*TZaFaNta*) for those that fear You" (Psalms

31:20). These good points blew on King David's harp, making melodies. Thus his harp played by itself, and in the same way, we can awaken at midnight from the heaviness of sleep.

The Exodus from Egypt also took place at midnight. After God informed Moses of the forthcoming Exodus, He commanded the Jewish People to sanctify the new moon. This was the very first commandment given to the Jewish People as they prepared to leave Egypt.

The redemption from Egypt came about because of the remaining good points of all the Jews in Egypt. They had become blemished and had fallen to the forty-ninth level of impurity, as it is written, "And I passed over you and I saw you weltering in your own blood" (Ezekiel 16:6). Nevertheless, God had pity on them and found their good points even in the depths of the Egyptian defilement that had overcome them. "I said to you, 'In your blood, live! In your blood, live!'" (ibid.). Even amidst the overwhelming blood and filth—despite it—God said, "Live!" For even there it is possible to find the good points.

Now we can understand why the very first commandment given to the Jewish nation was the sanctification of the moon. The sighting of even the smallest portion of the new moon—a modicum of good—is sufficient to proclaim the new month. Finding the modicum of good brought about the Egyptian redemption. And in the future, the same process will characterize the final redemption, when Israel's exiled will be gathered in from the nations of the world.

• Dividing the Night

Moses said to Pharaoh in God's name, "About midnight I will go out in the midst of Egypt" (Exodus 11:4). At midnight, the good point is aroused—and therefore the north wind blew at that time upon King David's harp. The "good wind" (which is the good point) emanates specifically from the north because the north is the place of evil, as it is written, "Out of the north the evil will break forth" (Jeremiah 1:14). When the good comes out of the very depths of evil, its greatness is most apparent. The best way to perceive light is in contrast to the darkness (*Zohar*, Introduction).

At midnight, the Shekhinah is at its diminution, as it were—it is no larger than a small point. Sleep is at its heaviest. At that time, all those whose hearts have been touched by the fear of Heaven must awaken and overcome their sleep. They do this with only a little bit of good to rely on.

This awakening parallels the Exodus from Egypt. God took pity on the Jews and passed over their houses when He brought the Plague of the Firstborn upon the Egyptians. In His mercy, the Holy One gathered all the good points of the Jews. The very concept of *Israel* alludes to the good points. Therefore God called the Jewish People, "My son, my firstborn, Israel" (Exodus 4:22). On the night of Pesach, Israel was *separated out* from the firstborn of the Egyptians and redeemed from the forces of the Other Side.

The first to reveal the secret power of midnight was Abraham. Abraham went to war against the four kings to rescue his nephew Lot from captivity (Genesis 14). When Abraham went into battle, "he divided the night against them" (ibid., 14:15). Breaking the heaviness of sleep and splitting the darkness of night with the good point can be accomplished only through the quality of lovingkindness embodied in Abraham, who always inclined towards the attribute of love. Abraham pursued the kings to save Lot because of the good point Lot possessed. Lot himself was wicked, yet Abraham risked his life to save him because Ruth was destined to be descended from Lot—therein lay Lot's good point. Ruth was the ancestor of King David and the Mashiach, who is the very root and essence of the good point.

The four kings really wanted to kill Lot. The repressive forces always seek to overpower the good point. But God does not abandon it to their hands. He gave enough strength to the power of love embodied in Abraham to save Lot through Lot's good point.

Therefore Abraham was able to overcome these mighty kings. By judging favorably and finding the good points even in the wicked, evil can be subdued. It only takes a little good to banish evil.

• The Exact Moment of Midnight

The Talmud records a difference of opinion among the Rabbis regarding the ability to determine the exact moment of midnight. The Talmud asks, "Did King David know the exact time of midnight? Even our teacher Moses did not know it. For it is written, "About midnight I will go out into the midst of Egypt" (Exodus 11:4).This seems to imply that David was not able to determine the exact moment. Comes the answer: "A harp hung above David's bed. As soon as midnight arrived, a north wind came and blew upon it, and [the harp] played by itself. [David] arose immediately and began studying Torah until daybreak" (*Berakhot* 3b).

Underlying this discussion is a theme that reaches the summit of Jewish destiny—the redemption of the Jewish People as a whole, and the personal redemption of each and every Jew. The essence of redemption depends on the skill of being able to determine the exact point of midnight. When the heaviness of "sleep" overtakes a Jewish soul, it threatens to overcome him completely, God forbid, due to his many sins and shortcomings. He is in danger of falling completely. But at precisely that moment, God in His mercy enlightens him, causing him to remember his good points and revive himself.

Rising at midnight demonstrates this redemptive process in action. At midnight, the Shekhinah—the embodiment of all the Jewish souls—is at her lowest, most minuscule point. Bitterly, she cries out to God, "Like the hart pants for brooks of water, so my soul pants for You, my God" (Psalms 42:2, included in the liturgy of *Tikkun Chatzot, Tikkun Leah*). "A voice is heard on high, lamentation and bitter weeping...Rachel weeping for her children" (Jeremiah 31:14, also included in the liturgy of *Tikkun Chatzot*). Then God arouses his mercy and extends a thread of lovingkindness towards her (See *Zohar Chadash*).

The same thing happens to each and every Jew, all the time. A Jew is constantly threatened by "sleep" until he comes to the verge of stumbling. This is the moment at which he must look for his good point, as we saw earlier. "If I said, 'My foot is slipping,' Your lovingkindness would sustain me. When my cares within me are many, Your comforts cheer my soul" (Psalms 94:18-19). This is the teaching of *Azamra!* When a person reaches the ultimate in constricted consciousness—when he wants to say, "My foot is slipping"—at that moment, God's love holds him up, rousing him from his sleep and supporting him. This is literally "getting up at midnight," which is the time of extreme constriction. At precisely this moment, one must arouse himself from sleep, rising from his fall through the teaching of *Azamra!*—"I will sing to my God with the little I have left."

Both the general and personal redemptions depend on this. And so we find that the first redemption of the Jewish People from Egypt took place at midnight. Similarly, the final redemption, which we hope will come speedily in our days, will also come about in the merit of "midnight"—the *Tikkun Chatzot*, the Midnight Lament, for which truly religious and God-fearing individuals rise up each night, drawing upon themselves the holiness of midnight, a time when great love is aroused.[9] This devotion empowers them to *always* awaken from their "sleep" at "midnight"— namely, the moment when a deep spiritual sleep threatens to engulf them. They may fall; all kinds of things may happen to them. No matter! They can still rouse themselves even from the very depths of their personal constrictions. Through the little bit of good they find, they can always wake up at their personal midnight.

---

9 In several communities today, individuals and groups practice this devotion every night.

• Moses, David, Mashiach

Why was Moses unable to determine the exact moment of midnight? The answer is that the Torah had not yet been given, so as yet, there was no "arousal from below." There were not yet that many Tzaddikim who rose at midnight to occupy themselves with Torah, because the Torah had not yet been given! Thus it was difficult to determine the exact moment of midnight. Even according to the opinion that Moses *did* know the exact moment but could not speak openly about it for fear that people would make mistakes, our explanation still stands. Moses could not yet reveal his insight to the world because the Torah had not yet been received in the world.

King David did know the exact moment because he had a harp hanging above his bed. We find in the teachings of Rebbe Nachman that the power of this harp derived from the Torah—its five strings corresponded to the five books of the Torah (see *Likutey Moharan* II, 8). Because this harp roused him from his sleep, David knew how to determine the exact moment of midnight.

King David is the embodiment of Mashiach, whose constantly task is to rectify Jewish souls, rousing them from their sleep through the good points he finds in them. He enlightens each person individually, guiding him to seek out his good points and awaken from his sleep so he will not fall completely. (See "The Burgher and the Pauper," *Rebbe Nachman's Stories* #10).

Most importantly, one must know how to determine the exact moment when he is on the verge of falling. At that instant, God will enlighten him with His love to save him and wake him up. "Though he falls, he will not be thrown down, for God upholds him" (Psalms 37:24). "The wicked man watches for the righteous, seeking to slay him. But God will not abandon him to his hand" (ibid., 37:32-33). These verses appear in the same Psalm as the verse that forms the foundation of the teaching of *Azamra!*: "And in but a little bit the sinner is not" (ibid., 37:10). It carries the same message for the Jewish People as a whole. "When He sees that their power is gone, with no protection or help; He will say: 'Where is their god, the rock in which they trusted?...See, now, that I, I am the only One! There are no gods with Me" (Deuteronomy 32:36-39).

Redemption is found in the power of the Torah—for today we have received the Torah. It was given to us through our teacher Moses and through all the Tzaddikim who lived until now and who explained the Torah's ways to us.

How did King David know when it was midnight? Through his harp, through his ability to *play*. Of

David it is written, "He *knows how to play*" (I Samuel 16:18). The entire lesson of *Azamra!* is expressed in the concept of the holy melodies emanating from King David's harp: *Azamra!*—"I will sing!" "Awake my glory, awake the lyre and the harp. I will awaken the dawn." Through these melodies, David knew how to determine the exact moment of midnight. King David is the Mashiach, through whom the final redemption will come about—the redemption that will end all exiles. It will come about through the "songs and melodies" of the "anointed of the Lord of Jacob, the sweet singer of Israel" (II Samuel 23:1). May he come speedily in our time. Amen.

Chidushim

Rebbe Nachman teaches that whenever a person studies Torah, he should endeavor to apply what he studies to himself. He should see himself in the words he is studying. Therefore, each individual has the power to apply his own insights to the Torah he studies, and further, to elaborate its meaning and implications. This is the concept of chidushim, new elaborations of Torah teachings. The leading Torah scholars among Rebbe Nachman's followers compiled their own chidushim on the Rebbe's teachings. The lesson of Azamra! generated a rich collection of explanatory material, selections of which appear in the following pages.

• Turning Black Into White?

The teaching of *Azamra!* does not imply that what is manifestly evil can be turned into good by finding a "good point" within it. Rebbe Nachman does not say that the evil a person does should be judged favorably. Elsewhere he taught, "A person who justifies an evildoer is also called evil" (*Sefer HaMidot, Harchakat Reshaim* 6). Rather, Rebbe Nachman urges us to find some good point that existed in the evildoer *previously*. In that place, this person is not evil, and then it is possible to judge him on the scale of merit. Every single Jew, no matter who he is, possesses at least some spark of the holiness of Israel within him—and the Jewish People are a part of Godliness, which is the source of all good. Therefore, it is impossible for a Jew to fall completely into evil and be a complete evildoer.

(*Biur HaLikutim* 282)

• Israel and Song

The Land of Israel contains the source of song and melody. Songs and melodies are made by sifting the good points that exist in each person—selecting the "good wind" or the good spirit—and rejecting the bad. The Land of Israel is the place for this process of sifting and selecting. Of this Land it is written, "From the corner of the *land* we heard *songs*" (Isaiah 24:16), and, "Let Your *good spirit* lead me in the *land* of righteousness" (Psalms 143:10). The Levites sang their daily song in the Land of Israel—in the Holy Temple, the Sanctuary where all the good points of all the Jewish People were collected. …For Jerusalem is called "good"—"this *good* mountain" (Deuteronomy 3:25)—and the Land of Israel is called "good" (Exodus 3:8, et al.). This Land is both "desirable and good"—desirable in the sense that all the good points crave and desire to be included there, just as they crave to be merged in the genuine prayer leader.

"The time of singing has arrived" (Song of Songs 2:12). This verse refers to the songs and melodies that are created after the good points have been gathered together and formed into the Sanctuary, from which the little schoolchildren receive the untainted breath of their mouths. The verse continues, "The voice of the turtledove is heard in our land" (ibid.). The *Zohar* explains, "This is the voice of the little schoolchildren learning Torah" (*Zohar* I, 1b). This voice is heard "in our land"—in the Land of Israel.

(*Zimrat HaAretz* 282)

• Shabbat

On Shabbat, everyone is judged favorably and all harsh judgments are overturned. Accordingly, the good point which is to be found in every Jew—even in sinners—shines forth on Shabbat. "There is no such thing as a Jewish sinner who does not have good deeds that elevate him to the World to Come. When do they elevate him? On Shabbat. Thus all are crowned with the crown of Shabbat" (*Zohar Chadash, Bereshit*). Similarly, the Rabbis commented on the verse, "I am black but comely" (Song of Songs 1:5): "I am black—on the weekdays, but comely—on Shabbat" (*Shir HaShirim Rabbah* 1:5). Since the good point shines forth on Shabbat, everyone is judged on the scale of merit on that day, and through this, they genuinely move onto the scale of merit and are able to return to God in true repentance. Thus *ShaBbaT* includes the concept of *TeShuVah*, repentance. Accordingly, the Sages said, "He who observes Shabbat is forgiven all his sins" (*Shabbat* 118b). This accounts for the great joy of Shabbat.

(*Kedushat Shabbat* 282)

• In Practice

Rebbe Nachman often said he wanted very much for us to follow his teachings in the sense of taking one of his lessons and concentrating on it for two or three months at a time. During that period, all our efforts towards spiritual advancement should be centered around the teachings in that lesson, and all our prayers and meditations should be directed towards achieving the concepts discussed therein. We should carry on with this for some time and then go on to another lesson, also for a few months. And so we should continue until we have gone through all the Rebbe's lessons. Happy is the man who takes this to heart.

(*Rebbe Nachman's Wisdom* #297)

Reb Noson once asked Rabbi Meir of Teplik about a man from Teplik who was somewhat attached to him. Rabbi Meir answered in a tone of indifference, as if to say the person in question wasn't much to talk about.

"Please listen to what I am going to tell you," said Reb Noson. "If you want to look at things negatively, you'll find fault with everyone in the whole world. See for yourself. Try to think of all the people you know living in your town. Start with the person living at the edge of the town. If you look at him carefully, you'll certainly find some shortcomings. Go from house to house until you get to *your* house. Are you the only good Jew in the whole town?"

"I'm also not such a good Jew," said Rabbi Meir.

"Then who is a good Jew?" asked Reb Noson. "If you would try to look at the world positively, then even when you look at the worst of people, you'll be able to find at least something good. And you certainly will [find good] when you think about the people who aren't so bad. This applies to everyone. Even in *you* there's something good. If you look at things this way, you'll be able to improve the whole world."

(*Parparaot LeChokhmah* 282, end)

Another time, Reb Noson was speaking about this path of *Azamra!* Rabbi Nachman of Tulchin was sitting by as Reb Noson discussed the whole subject. In his passionate thirst for Reb Noson's sweet words, Rabbi Nachman repeated every word after him, under his breath. Reb Noson asked him, "Do you think this is a simple, easy matter? I will explain to you what is so hard about it. Do not forget: the Rebbe said that by judging ourselves and others favorably, we really do elevate ourselves onto the scale of merit and can then return to God. If it were within our power to achieve this, we would be able to bring the entire world back to God."

(*Parparaot LeChokhmah* 282)

Reb Noson writes:

The Rebbe told me he had been speaking with someone who was complaining bitterly about how terrible his behavior was. This man wanted very much to draw closer to God and change his behavior for the better. But each time he tried, the temptations grew stronger and stronger. The days had turned into years and he had still not managed to extricate himself from his bad ways. But each time he would try even harder to control himself, and was always struggling to get closer to God.

As he complained to the Rebbe about how terrible his behavior was, the Rebbe answered him with great wisdom. He said in a tone of sincerity and simplicity, "I have no one to speak to because everything is totally bad." At this, the man got excited and said to the Rebbe, "But I do try to fight back at times and get closer to what I should be as a Jew." "Only the slightest bit," answered the Rebbe. He then told the man to make it a practice to follow the teaching of *Azamra!*

I understood the Rebbe to mean that this was precisely how he revived this man. He had already fallen so low in his own sight that it was not possible to revive him with anything. It was only when the Rebbe told him that he was totally bad that he was startled and became excited. It was then that he started feeling a little of the holiness of the good points that were still to be found in him. Then the Rebbe advised him to follow the lesson of *Azamra!*

(*Chayey Moharan, Avodat HaShem* 118)

Rebbe Nachman told his followers to "turn the lessons into prayers" (Likutey Moharan II, 25). *His prescription acknowledged the integral relationship between prayer and study in the spiritual life of a Jew. With the Rebbe's encouragement, Reb Noson wrote extensive prayers based on the lessons in Likutey Moharan, which he collected and published in Likutey Tefilot. The following is Reb Noson's prayer to fulfill the teaching of Azamra!*

Reb Noson's Prayer
Likutey Tefilot I, 90

"I will praise God with my life; I will sing to my God with the little I have left."

(Psalms 146:2)

Master of the Universe, help me! You work in amazing ways; Your love is so powerful. Help me to be able to make myself happy at all times. I am shattered and broken. Help me be happy always.

• Teach Me a Way

You and You alone know all things:

You know everything that has happened from the day the first man was created until today.

You know everything that is happening to this generation, and everything taking place in the world as a whole and in all the souls of the Jewish People.

You know what *I* am going through—a poor, degraded, ruined sinner. Even to myself I am cruel.

You know everything that has happened to my soul: from the day my *neshamah*, *ruach* and *nefesh* were first emanated; how they descended through the worlds of *Atzilut*, *Beriah*, *Yetzirah* and *Asiyah*; how they were brought into all the bodies in which they were incarnated until they entered this body of mine, this gross and materialistic body.

You know all that has happened to me since the day that the exalted elder[10] remembers—he who remembers nothing—and since the times which the other holy elders can remember—those who remember the appearance, the taste and the smell; and how the Sages produced the seed; and the time when they brought forth the seed to plant the fruit; the time when the fruit began to form; the time when the light was kindled; and the time when they cut the fruit from the tree. …

You alone know the meaning of all these mysteries and all that happened to me in those times and since then until today.

You know all that I have done, the good and the bad. You know all my sins and transgressions, day by day—those that were unintentional and those I did deliberately; those I did under compulsion and those I did of my own free will.

And You also know whatever good points I have managed to gather. It was only through Your kindness that I did so—even in the bad times I have endured from the day I was born until today.

And now, after all this, after everything that has happened to me and after everything I have done, good or bad—guide me and teach me a way I can take from

---

10 See *Rebbe Nachman's Stories* #13, p. 363, for a full explanation of this paragraph.

now on, a way of truth. Then I will be able to return to You truthfully from now on.

• The Good Points

Master of the Universe, Your desire is for love. You are filled with kindness. When a person does evil, You wait for him, hoping he will return. You constantly judge all people on the scale of merit. You are abundant in love, ever doing good. You govern the world with love and deal kindly with all Your creatures.

Help me and bring me to follow the path of truth. Even after all that has happened, let me search out and find some merit in myself, a few good points, and constantly judge myself on the scale of merit. Then I will be able to return to You in perfect repentance, and through this I will be able to pray with inner concentration, life and passion, with true happiness and joy. I will truly be able to "sing to my God with the little I have left."

• There is Hope

Master of the Universe, what life is there for me, what strength or hope do I have, how will I ever be able to open my mouth and speak before You, if not through following the profound and awesome path of holiness which our Rabbis revealed in the words of the Psalm, "I will sing to my God with the little I have left"?

Likutey Tefilot • 75

You know the damage I have caused by my sins. You know what they were, how many they were, and how serious they were. You know, too, the pain of those sins. There should be almost no hope for me at all; from head to toe, I am all sores, wounds and bruises.

Yet You have taught us that we must search for the good points in ourselves and through them make ourselves happy. We must never become discouraged or fall into despair. Not in any way.

So help me. Teach me the way to achieve this.

I get so discouraged and depressed because of all the terrible things I have done. There are times when the depression overwhelms me. The most negative thoughts come into my mind, eating away at me and breaking my determination, as if to say, "There is no hope for you!"

This is when I need Your help, God of love—to fight back with all my strength and refuse to be discouraged in any way. At those moments, help me throw myself with all my strength into searching for my good points—all the good things You have helped me do throughout my life until today.

Because however degraded and lowly we may be after all the wrong we've done, You never abandon us, loving God. At all times, You enable us to accomplish at least something good, some mitzvah or good deed, even when things are very bad. For this You praise the Community of Israel, sunken as we are in exile and degradation: "Your temples are like a pomegranate split open" (Song of Songs 4:3). Just as a pomegranate is full of seeds, so even the Jewish sinners are full of mitzvot.

Maybe the way we do the mitzvot is far from perfect. We do them with impure motives and negative thoughts, and constantly succumb to all sorts of distractions. We may not have performed even a single mitzvah perfectly. Even so, it isn't possible that the things we did lacked any good points. Everyone has done at least some mitzvah at one time or another—wearing tzitzit or tefilin, keeping Shabbat and Festivals, avoiding forbidden foods, giving charity or doing someone a kindness. …Every single mitzvah and every good deed contains a good point!

So no matter what else might have happened in our lives, these good points are something for us to be happy about, all our days and forever.

We may be very low. Yet these good points of ours brought You pleasure, and this is something we can be happy about. Through this, we can truthfully move onto the scale of merit and make ourselves happy at all times. Then we can return to You in true repentance.

I believe with perfect faith that through the wonderful path of *Azamra!*—a channel of *love*—there is hope

Likutey Tefilot • 77

for me, too. There is hope for even the worst sinners of Israel to return to You and be constantly happy.

• Judging Others Favorably

Also bring me to judge *others* on the scale of merit at all times.

Even when I see someone who is completely evil, I will still search until I find some good points in him. I will keep trying until I succeed in judging him on the scale of merit. Through this, I can truthfully elevate him onto the scale of merit and bring him to repent completely and return to You.

Master of the World, the true Tzaddikim constantly intercede for the Jewish People and speak in their defense. They continually dig down and search until they find merit and goodness in every single Jew, even the very worst. Through the merit and strength of these Tzaddikim, let me accomplish this, too.

• Closeness to the Tzaddikim

Let me draw closer to these true Tzaddikim, who in their wisdom find the good points in every person. They gather these good points together, one by one, until they have found a number of them. They elevate even sinners onto the scale of merit. Out of all these good points, they build holy edifices of awesome wonder. All this brings You great pleasure, pleasure like no other since the beginning of time. And by gathering together the good points from even the darkest places, the Tzaddikim create holy melodies and songs.

Master of the Universe, God of kindness, let me draw closer to these Tzaddikim and become a part of them. Let me hear their holy prayer, for they alone know how to pray for the entire Jewish People, to stand at the reader's desk and enable the entire congregation to fulfill its obligation for prayer. Gathering together the good points in each individual, they pray before You with all this good and turn Your severity into love.

God of love and kindness, let us be included in the prayers of these Tzaddikim, so that they might always pray for us. May they give You no rest until You take pity on us, each one of us, gathering us to You and bringing us *home*, elevating us onto the scale of merit and gladdening our souls at all times. Then You will bring us to return to You in perfect repentance from now and forever.

• A Prayer for Our Children

Also take pity on us, on our children and on all the children of Your People, the House of Israel.

Guard and protect our Jewish children and save them from the evil influences that are spreading throughout the world because of our sins, as You know. Protect our children from unbelievers. Some people have fallen completely under the influence of alien ideas. They would have our children educated according to *their* ideas, distancing them from the Torah traditions we have received. Even if they have a place for the Torah, they try to distort its meaning and restrict the time spent on it as much as they can.

Protect our children from the mockers who think they are so clever and who scorn those who have chosen the path of simplicity—to work for God and to follow His Torah in the way we have received from our fathers and teachers. Many have risen up against those who follow this way of justice, spreading a net for their feet to trap them and turn them astray.

God, You know all this! You know how these influences are weakening our attachment to You! Have pity on us and on our children and on all the children of Your People, the House of Israel. Guard and save our children from the evil influences that threaten them at an age when they are most vulnerable. Help us and protect us always. Guide us and teach us to know at all times how we should bring up our children and grandchildren from their earliest days. How we can protect them and save them from these harmful influences, and teach them to follow Your paths of holiness and truth for good. How we can make sure that they will always walk the path of justice and truth with purity and simplicity, following Your will in the way we have received from our fathers and Rabbis.

Help us make known to all our children and to the generations that will succeed us, all the mighty acts of God that You have performed for us in each generation from the days of our fathers until today. Let us instill in them this knowledge so strongly that future generations will also know and tell it to *their* children. Then we will fulfill the words of the Torah, "And you shall make it known to your children and your children's children" (Deuteronomy 4:9), imbuing them with the holiness of our pure and perfect faith.

Show love to the children of Your People from their earliest days, so that they might receive the pure, untainted breath of their mouths from the holy tents of the true Tzaddikim. Each Tzaddik builds a holy sanctuary which is the source of the holy breath of the little schoolchildren.

• The Breath Without Sin

Master of the Universe, You know all that is happening to the little schoolchildren in the world in our generation. The whole world endures only through the untainted breath of their mouths. But many are rising up to spoil and corrupt them from the days of their youth.

Take pity on the children and on us, for Your sake!

Protect them and guard them from all harmful influences. You, God, guard them from this time and forever. Have pity on the last remnants of the children of Your People, the House of Israel.

We have nothing to depend on, save the untainted breath of their mouths. Show love to them and to us, so that every single Jewish child will receive the breath of his mouth from the holy sanctuary of the true Tzaddik to whom he is bound at the root of his soul. Then each child will go forward, learn to serve God, and enter the Torah in truth. Let them learn Torah for its own sake and meditate on it day and night. Let their hearts be opened in the study of Your Torah, and give their hearts understanding to grow wise; hearing, learning and teaching to observe, do and fulfill all the words of Your Torah in love. Enlighten their eyes in Your Torah and bind their hearts with Your mitzvot. Lengthen their days and years for good and for pleasantness. Be with them always and help them serve You in truth all their days and forever.

• In the Merit of the Tzaddikim

Master of the Universe, You are filled with love. You know all that is hidden.

Let us accomplish what we ask of You through the merit and strength of the great Tzaddikim, who work constantly to judge the entire world on the scale of merit and to search out the good points in every single Jew, even the lowest. They gather all this good together and come with it before You in prayer to sweeten and nullify all the harsh judgments in the world.

These great Tzaddikim understand what is at stake with the little schoolchildren, both in general and in every detail. They "see where the schoolchildren are reading" and they understand from which Tzaddik each child draws the untainted breath of his mouth. They understand how many receive from each Tzaddik and all that is involved in this, and they see the generations that will come from these children until the end of days. Through the merit and strength of these Tzaddikim, help us and our children, the children of Your People, the House of Israel. Fulfill what we have asked of You for good and with love.

• True Happiness

Master of the World, let me truly move onto the scale of merit so that I will be able to return to You in true repentance from now on.

In the merit of all the true Tzaddikim who have lived in each generation, and in the merit of all the true Tzaddikim in this generation, help me. Guide me and teach me. At all times, give me good and true advice as to how I can always make myself happy by following the path of *Azamra!*

Likutey Tefilot • 83

Let me never allow depression to enter or even so much as touch me. Let me always be happy—truly happy, with all my heart and soul. Put joy into my heart through following the path of *Azamra!* so I will always be only happy—happy over every single good point inside me. Also, help me bring others to happiness. Guide me and instill me with the awareness and understanding to bring joy to Jewish souls at all times, and to judge them on the scale of merit. Then they will return to You in truth and joy.

Speedily fulfill the words of the prophet: "I will give them one heart and place a new spirit within them, and I will remove the heart of stone from their flesh and give them a heart of flesh; so they will walk in My statutes and fulfill My judgments, and they will be My people and I will be their God" (Ezekiel 11:19-20).

Let us serve God with joy and come before Him in exultation, fulfilling the words of the Psalm: "Let Israel rejoice in their Maker; let the children of Zion exult in their King" (Psalms 149:2).

"I will sing to God with my life; I will sing to my God with the little I have left. Let my meditation be sweet to Him; I will rejoice in God. The sinners will disappear from the earth, the wicked are no longer. Let my soul bless God. *Hallelu-Yah*" (Psalms 104:33-35).

∼

Once there was a fire in the town of Breslov. Afterwards, Reb Noson and a few others went to see where the fire had been. Reb Noson saw the man whose house had burned down crying terribly and looking to see if he could salvage any pieces of wood or metal to rebuild his house. He was collecting the pieces one by one.

Reb Noson said to his companions, "Did you see? Even though his house has burned down, he hasn't given up hope of rebuilding it. He's collecting everything he'll need when it comes to rebuilding. The same is true in spiritual life. The Evil One battles with us to the point that he almost burns us up completely. But we must never give up hope. We must pick up a few good points and gather them together from amidst the numerous sins. This is the way to return to God."